IDENTIFYING AMERICAN BRILLIANT CUT GLASS

IDENTIFYING
AMERICAN
BRILLIANT
CUT GLASS

Bill and Louise Boggess

CROWN PUBLISHERS, INC.
NEW YORK

Dedicated to
the many who helped us
research this book

Published by Crown Publishers, Inc., One Park Avenue, New York, New
York 10016, and simultaneously in Canada by General Publishing
Company Limited

Manufactured in the United States of America

LIBRARY OF CONGRESS CATALOGING IN PUBLICATION DATA

Boggess, Bill.
Identifying American brilliant cut glass.

Bibliography: p.
Includes indexes.
1. Cut glass—United States—History.
I. Boggess, Louise.   II. Title.
NK5203.B64   1984   748.2913   83-7733
ISBN 0-517-55009-1
ISBN 0-517-55010-5 (pbk.)

Designed by Rhea Braunstein

10 9 8 7 6 5 4 3 2 1
First Edition

Contents

Acknowledgments

WE greatly appreciate the personal assistance in research given by Virginia Wright, assistant librarian, Corning Museum; Wallace Turner, founder of the Stepping Stone Inn (Tuthill Museum); Anne O. Reece, librarian, Toledo Museum of Art; Charles G. Berger, reference librarian, Museum of American History; George C. Avila, associated with New Bedford Museum; and Robert W. Harper III, director, and Irene Miller of Lightner Museum.

We have obtained additional information from Wayne County Historical Museum in Honesdale, Pennsylvania; Sandwich Glass Museum in Sandwich, Massachusetts; Chrysler Museum in Norfolk, Virginia; Old State House in Little Rock, Arkansas; and Eberhart Museum in Scranton, Pennsylvania.

The late Louis Iorio, Bill Iorio, Miss Lucille Egginton, and Donald Parsche provided information on patterns, cutting procedures, and personal insights, readily answering our numerous questions.

A special thanks goes to Pauline Guetta for research on Canadian glass, Robert Blake Powell for assistance with barber bottles, Barbara Shea for advertisements on cut glass from old magazines, to Vickie and Tom Matthews for expert advice on repairs, and Robert Loomis for sketches of signatures.

We wish to personally thank these friends for their help: Jack and Duncan McRae, Isabelle and Robert Middleton, and Doris and B. B. Eiland.

We expressly extend our appreciation to the following who shared information and/or invited us to photograph their collections:

Mrs. Samuel Abramson
Margaret and H. G. Alexander
Ian Berke
Mr. and Mrs. K. G. Bernard
S. Bernstein
Lila Bloomfield

Dr. and Mrs. R. F. Borrelli, Jr.
Gary Brewer
Sheldon Butts
Barbara Chamberlin
Lucy and Fred Cornett
Cottage Antiques

Nancy Cross
Joseph Cummings
Mrs. Paul R. Davis
Duke Dobbs
Carolyn and Mike Dolecheck
Pam and Paul Donath
Tom Duncan
Tom Dunshee
Jack Farmer
Jackie Fishel
Helen Tuthill Gardiner
Kitty Gibbs
Beverly and Herman Gierow
Ralph Girkins
Frank Goularte
Dale Green
Joe Gyenes
Dr. Jon Hall
Connie and Gordon Harwood
Jim Haven
Ida Hayden
Florence and Vincent Helpling
Peter Herring
Joyce and Jack Horton
Alfred Huddleston
Jean and Hugh Huff
Bob Hunt
Bill Johns
Beverly Johnson
Robert D. Joyce
Berl Kaiserman
Keith Kinkade
Wanda and Stewart Kipper
Rita Klyce
Harry Kraut
Mr. and Mrs. Roger Larson
La Tournous Cut Glass
R. J. LaTournous Cut Glass
Grace and Ray Lefarver
Robert Lehmann
Marcia and Malcolm Longaker
Laudy Lopes
Howard McFarland

Mary McKinley
Frances McRae
Terri McRae
John E. Mayer
Carol Miller
Larry Milot
Duane Mumson
Gerald Noll
Mary Obblink
Alice Otten
Mary Patterson
Roscoe Penrod
Gladys Pressman
John S. Prickett, Jr.
Jean Quigley
Richard Quigley, Jr.
Mildred Quinn
Joan and Richard Randles
Jane and Max Redden
Lynne and Irving Rosen
Harold Rothberg
Frank Russo
Charnee and George Schatel
Joyce and Sam Shrighley
Shulls Pianos and Antiques
Evelyn and Tom Sisk
Dr. and Mrs. John R. Sisk
Comdr. F. E. Smetheram, USNR
Mr. and Mrs Bernie Smith
Joanie and Bill Spencer
Pat Steward
Louise Swan
Lorene and Alex Tisnado
Bettye W. Waher
Florence Taylor Vay
Jim Weisbrod
Dallas Wertzberger
Arthur Wilk
Jean and James Wilson
Henrietta Wise
Ellsworth Young
Mr. and Mrs. Kenneth Zimmerman
Dorothy and Milton C. Zink

Finally, we sincerely thank the many dealers who shared information with us and the collectors who wrote us about their cut glass.

Preface

THE publication of our book, *American Brilliant Cut Glass*, has alerted us to a keen interest in the identification of cut glass. We have received letters, telephone calls, and talked with numerous dealers and collectors. All want information about source, pattern, or function of pieces of cut glass. Because of this growing interest, we decided to make identification of cut glass patterns and shapes the general theme of this second book.

Within recent years many old cut glass catalogs have become available. Some of these have neither a number nor a date. The Corning Museum Library has also restored those damaged by a flood. When the catalog pages became separated in the restoration process, the library put those of T. G. Hawkes & Company under an approximate date and grouped those of the Pairpoint Corporation by function of items. The style of printing and a few original page numbers indicate fourteen catalogs in the Hawkes group. The Pairpoint group furnished no clues as to the number of catalogs combined. Rather than approximate a date for such catalogs, we have identified the patterns by company name only.

The educational program of reprinting old cut glass catalogs, undertaken by the American Cut Glass Association, has provided additional information on cut glass companies and patterns. The association has made these catalog reprints available to the general public.

We have based much of the information in this book on an intensive study of approximately one hundred catalogs. For the majority of our identifications, we relied on these catalogs, magazine advertisements, patent records, silver hallmarks, and signatures. We have made a few probable identifications by matching an unsigned piece to a signed one.

In addition to this information, we have learned many unrecorded facts about the Brilliant Period from people who worked in the industry, cut glass dealers we interviewed, and numerous collectors who wrote us.

In referring to factories or cutting shops, we have stated the full company name when first mentioned. After that we have referred to them by the name of the man who headed the company, such as Hawkes or Libbey, or a shortened form such as Empire or Quaker City. In discussing functions or shapes of pieces, we have listed the various names companies applied and from then on called the item by the most-used term.

From time to time we found descriptive names given to unknown patterns and unique functions attributed to certain items. In the text of this book we have placed such incorrect names and functions in quotation marks.

We have earnestly tried to accurately match photographs of cut glass to every detail of illustrations in catalogs, magazine advertisements, or sketches in patent records. If we made any errors—and we could very easily—we honestly tried.

By no means do we consider research on cut glass patterns complete. Tomorrow will bring more information in the form of another old catalog and add new pattern identifications. One fact will never change: the United States produced the finest cut glass in the world!

What is really beautiful needs no adorning.
SATAKA

IDENTIFYING AMERICAN BRILLIANT CUT GLASS

1

What Is It?

TODAY the identification of patterns and shapes in American Brilliant cut glass has become of prime importance to the collector and the dealer. They want to provide the correct answer when someone comments, "Pretty, but what is it?"

Within the last few years strong interest in American cut glass has stimulated museums, clubs, and associations to locate and preserve material of this era. The availability of old cut glass catalogs has done much to identify shapes by the correct names.

In the past, when collectors or dealers did not know the catalog name for a shape, they used a present-day term, such as "pitcher" for jug (1). If they found no comparable term, they borrowed a name from other types of glassware, china, or ceramics, such as "casserole" for covered bonbon (2). A few did considerable research to find a shape from the past that slightly resembled the item.

When all else failed, they improvised a descriptive name or an unusual but believable function for the shape. A collector showed us a round "butter press." "You decorate the top of a mound of butter by pressing this pattern on it," he explained. A Pairpoint Corporation catalog showed the identical shape as a doorknob (3).

Even original owners of cut glass created new functions for old shapes no longer stylish and passed this identification on to the heir or the buyer. A friend, for instance, showed us a small cylinder piece on a foot. "I love this little bud vase," she said. "My grandmother always kept a single rose in it."

According to old catalogs, she owned a hatpin holder—not a bud vase (4). Like all of us, she disliked changing what she had believed for so long—even though she owned a rarer shape than a bud vase. Of course, the authentic name may also identify a less rare piece.

Any incorrect identification creates unnecessary confusion when it continues in use. We believe in calling an old piece of cut glass by the name provided in the catalogs and used during the era. Some names, such as bonbon

1. A jug with a silver rim and blunt lip.

2. A covered bonbon with a thistle motif.

3. A doorknob called a "butter press."

4. A hatpin holder identified as a bud vase.

5. A nappy sometimes called a bonbon.

6. A spoon tray later called pickle dish or bonbon.

and nappy, do sound quaint, but they characterize the Brilliant Period of American cut glass.

The Brilliant Period began in 1876 when a number of companies introduced this prismatic glass at the Centennial Exposition in Philadelphia. The Exposition marked the end of dependency on Europe for designs and the creation of American patterns. During the next forty years the Americans produced the finest cut glass in the world. Unfortunately, around 1916, events began to involve the United States in World War I. Lead so essential for cut glass blanks went to make ammunition. Although a few companies lingered in business some years longer, the Brilliant Period more or less ended. We can recapture its glory by learning more about the period, beginning with old catalogs.

FACTS ABOUT CATALOGS

During the Brilliant Period, factories, cutting shops, retailers, and wholesalers published cut glass catalogs. A factory blew the blank and cut it. The cutting shop bought the blank from the factory and only cut it. The retailer and wholesaler bought the finished product from either a factory or a cutting shop.

Most catalogs followed the same basic organization and gave the same practical information. They listed general categories of shapes, such as bowls or celeries, at the top or bottom of a page. The specific information under the illustration normally gave the pattern name, order number, and price. A few catalogs included the size. The shape in many cases indicated the function, such as a sugar and cream set. At times a catalog listed two functions for a shape, such as olive or pin tray.

A page illustrating a variety of shapes dropped any general classification. A few companies, such as O. F. Egginton Company, omitted all general headings and gave only individual facts about the shapes. Occasionally companies did differ slightly on a name for a similar shape. One company might call a piece a nappy and another describe the same shape as a bonbon (5). When a shape when out of style, a later catalog would designate a new function. A spoon tray, for example, became a pickle dish or bonbon (6).

The following information based on catalogs currently available (see Bibliography) provided the most popular names for shapes and a few of the interesting exceptions from specific companies. No doubt new material from the past will add other information on special shapes.

PLENTIFUL SHAPES

Companies cut a number of shapes in abundance. Any person who owns a few pieces of cut glass most likely has a bowl, celery, or vase. Other plentiful shapes included jug, oil, or nappy.

BOWLS

Many of you own a fruit, salad, or berry bowl, 8–10 inches in diameter and 3½ inches in depth (7). The same shaped bowl that measures 6–7 inches sometimes gets identified as a "small berry bowl" instead of whipped cream (8). While companies produced a large number of berry bowls, they also offered a selection of shallow ones, 8–10 inches in diameter and 2–2½ inches in depth. Catalogs identified these shapes as low or nappy bowls (9). Occasionally, companies added two handles to this low bowl (10), but do not confuse this shape with the caboret.

A caboret, also round and shallow, added two handles and glass dividers for compartments (11). While T. B. Clark & Company and Libbey Glass Company named this shape a caboret, others merely referred to it as a compartment bowl.

The catalogs listed an oblong bowl, 10–14 inches, as oval, nut, or orange, and not as "banana" (12). While companies did produce a few footed ones (13), they made the majority footless.

To distinguish the same size fancy or fancy fruit bowls from the oval, nut, or orange, look for the lowered ends (14). You have possibly heard this shape called by the descriptive name of "Napoleon's Hat," not a catalog term.

Companies cut other deep and shallow bowls in the following shapes: square (15), triangle (16), hexagon (17), bell, and globe. T. G. Hawkes & Company did much to popularize the crimp or crimped bowl, devised by pincering to form a wavy edge (18). While C. G. Alford & Company listed such shapes as fluted, none of the available catalogs used the descriptive term of "blowout."

7. A 10-inch berry bowl with hobstar dominance.

8. An unusual whipped cream bowl with a silver rim.

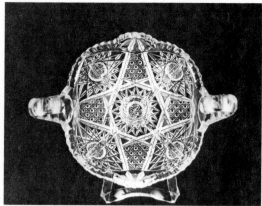

9. A low or nappy bowl, 10 inches in diameter with a 40-point hobstar in the center.

10. An 8-inch low bowl with two handles.

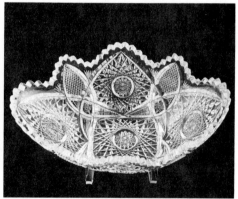

11. A 9-inch caboret or divided bowl with hobstar dominance.

12. A 12-inch oval nut or orange bowl with hobstar dominating.

13. A 12-inch oval bowl with a foot.

14. A 14½-inch fancy fruit bowl in hobstars and nailhead diamonds.

15. A 16-inch square salad bowl.

16. An 8-inch, Russian-cut low bowl in the shape of a triangle.

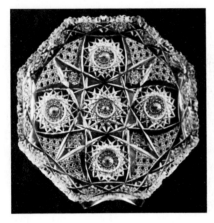

17. A low bowl in a hexagon shape.

18. A crimp bowl in Russian by Hawkes.

CELERY

The celery or celery tray measured 11–14 inches in length and 3½–5 inches in width. The craftsman cut the celery with three types of rims: straight sawtooth, scalloped sawtooth, or rolled sawtooth (19). We have heard the wider and differently shaped celery called a "bread tray" (20). Companies did make bread trays but somewhat wider (21). J. D. Bergen Company listed a shallow rectangular tray, 11½ by 7 inches, as a cake or bread tray. Taylor Brothers pictured an oval tray of approximately the same size for bread. Several collectors showed us a celery they identified as a "tablespoon tray" (22). The catalogs pictured only small spoon trays, 6–8 inches in length. L. Straus & Sons labeled this shape a celery (23).

19. An 11-inch celery with a scalloped, sawtooth rim.

20. A celery frequently mistaken for a bread tray.

21. A bread tray measuring 11½ by 6½ inches.

22. A celery often identified as a tablespoon tray.

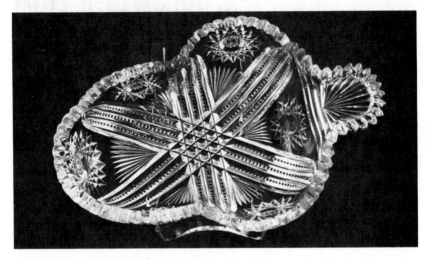

23. A unique shape in a celery.

JUG

Most of the early catalogs described "pitchers" as jugs. Information under the illustration generally gave the capacity, a half pint to a half gallon, rather than the height. The companies made most of the tall jugs for wine, a custom borrowed from Europe. The so-named Rhenish and Flemish jugs probably copied the shapes of ones made in those areas. Mt. Washington Glass Works offered juniper and schoffer jugs.

In addition to capacity, jugs differed among individual companies in shape, such as tall (24), squat (25), or fancy (26). Elmira Cut Glass Company pictured a tankard or tall jug as low or tall flange. C. Dorflinger & Sons added a long lip for a tusk jug in contrast to the usual blunt one most contained. All companies made champagne, claret, and lemonade jugs. The latter possibly catered to teetotalers.

The classification of pitcher generally appeared, if at all, in catalogs published late in the Brilliant Period. In the catalogs "pitcher" described certain shapes only, such as a small tankard (27) or globe (28). Although we could not substantiate this theory, we suspect the term "pitcher" implied Americanization.

24. A tall jug with a tusk lip.

25. A squat jug.

26. A shape identified in the catalogs as fancy jug.

27. A small tankard pitcher.

28. A globe-shaped pitcher.

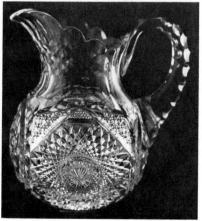

OIL

The early catalogs called the present-day "cruet" an oil. A 1904 Bergen catalog used the term oil on one page and cruet on the next for the same shape. Most oils held one-half pint. They may have a triple or single lip. You will find them in such shapes as globe (29), tall (30), footed, or flat based.

Because a few oils came with a flat base, someone described them as "ship" or "captain" cruets. While the catalogs pictured decanters, carafes, oils, and other shapes with flat bases, none labeled them "captain" or "ship" (31). Two references did indicate the use of the flat-based pieces on yachts. C. F. Monroe Company offered a carafe and tumbler similar to a guest set for a yacht. A Dorflinger advertisement in *Harper's* magazine for 1898 pictured flat-based glassware aboard a yacht.

29. An oil in a globe shape and three lips, the Wylie pattern by Blackmer.

30. An oil 9 inches tall.

31. A carafe with a flat base and rather odd shape.

VASE

In the catalogs, vases normally measured from 5 to 20 inches in height. Most companies considered the foot an integral part of certain shapes. Consequently no catalog called attention to a facet-cut knob, a scalloped foot (32), or a paperweight base (33). A few illustrations referred to tappan and trumpet vases. The tappan vase contained a smooth, flared rim, while the trumpet crimped the flared edge (34).

33. An 8-inch vase with a paperweight base.

32. A vase 8 inches tall with a facet cut knob on stem and scalloped foot.

34. A trumpet vase 10½ inches tall.

Other shapes described included cylinder, globe, revolving, and two-handled (35). The "corset" vase—a descriptive term—certainly resembled the body of a woman tightly laced, but no catalog used that name for a cylinder vase that bulged at the top and bottom. We have seen several tubular shapes, 20 or more inches tall—some with silver rims—identified as "cane stands" or "umbrella stands" (36). The catalogs did not identify any "stands." A dealer showed us a very beautiful 25-inch vase cut by Hawkes in the Albion pattern. It contained an inside, silver fitting you could adjust to the length of the flower stems.

Most of you will recognize a flower center, a shape also identified as a center vase (37). Companies produced them in sizes of 8, 10, and 12 inches. Some flower centers came in two parts and others with handles and a special foot (38). In the catalogs, violet describes a vase, globe, or holder. Since the small violet vase has the same shape as the flower center, some wrongly described it as a "miniature flower center" (39).

An old cutter told us that a rose globe or ball did not hold flowers but dried petals. Then a collector showed us one with a liner (40). Perhaps the liner explains why Libbey listed the same shape as a flower globe and Straus called it flowerbowl. Bergen added three handles to a small rose ball (41), but do not confuse this shape with a little loving cup (42). The loving cup differed from the rose ball in shape and an occasional silver rim. You may have heard the small loving cup incorrectly called a "demitasse spooner."

35. An 8-inch, two-handled vase.

36. A 20-inch vase with a silver rim sometimes wrongly identified as a cane stand or holder.

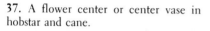

37. A flower center or center vase in hobstar and cane.

38. A footed flower or fruit center with handles.

39. A violet vase in pattern A. G. by Clark.

40. A 5-inch rose ball with a clear liner.

41. A 3-handled rose ball in Electric by Bergen.

42. A small loving cup with three handles and a silver rim.

SIMILAR SHAPES

Companies produced a number of shapes, both large and small, so similar that you can easily confuse them. A study of each shape does show one or more characteristics that eliminate the confusion and provide a specific identification.

BONBON

The bonbon (also spelled bon bon and bon-bon) described a small shallow piece, 3½–7½ inches in diameter, with no standard shape. It took such shapes as squares, hexagons, triangles, ovals, or leaves. One added a shaped handle (43) or a place for the thumb (44). A few catalogs designated shallow baskets for bonbons.

Sets of small pieces shaped as hearts, diamonds, spades, and clubs most catalogs described as bonbons (45), but Libbey identified them as nappies. You probably have heard them referred to as "bridge sets," a very descriptive name. F. X. Parsche & Sons Company described the set as a Euchre prize.

Catalogs listed the round shape with a lid as candy box, candy holder, or covered bonbon (46). Several people have described this shape as a "collar holder." One person even placed a man's celluloid collar in a bonbon to show how perfectly it fit, thereby supporting the identification.

Most of you will recognize a "stick dish," another descriptive term, but the catalogs identified this shape as a butter receiver, butter ball holder, bonbon, or confection dish (47). A 5-inch shape with no lapidary knob on the post has been called a "miniature stick dish." The catalogs listed the shape as a ring or jewel stand with a post, ring tree, ring holder, or ring tray (48).

43. A bonbon with a handle that forms a part of the shape.

44. A bonbon with a place to put the thumb when holding, in Starling pattern by Blackmer.

45. The diamond from a four-piece set of bonbons incorrectly identified as a bridge set.

46. A candy box with a buzzstar dominance.

47. A bonbon or butter ball holder.

48. A 3-inch ring holder or tray.

NAPPY

As a rule, a nappy had a round shape that measured 5–6 inches in diameter. Most nappies came with one (49) or no handles (50), but companies produced them with two (51) or three (52). One collector owns a rare divided nappy with only one handle (53).

SETS

Many berry bowls came in sets with matching saucers, 5–6 inches in diameter and 1½ inches in depth (54). Another popular set included an ice cream tray and matching shallow plates, 5–6 inches in diameter (55). Some companies likewise matched saucers instead of plates to the ice cream tray. As a rule, many companies offered the saucer (56) or the plate (57) with a handle like a nappy. These get mistaken for nappies. Tuthill Cut Glass Company cut only saucers and plates—no nappies.

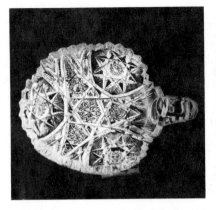

49. A 6-inch nappy with one handle and flashed star dominant motif.

50. A 6-inch nappy with no handle in Seymour by Bergen.

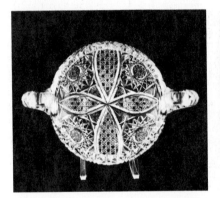

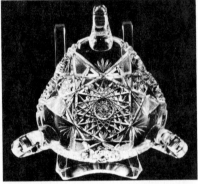

51. A 7-inch, two-handled nappy.

52. A 5-inch nappy with three handles.

53. A divided nappy with only one handle.

54. A 5-inch saucer that went with a berry bowl or ice cream tray.

55. A 7-inch plate that matched an ice cream tray.

56. A 5-inch saucer with a handle.

57. A 6-inch plate with a handle, Huyler pattern and signed Clark.

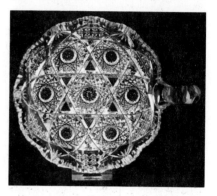

DISH

Companies used the term dish to describe a hodgepodge of large shapes. Several catalogs listed a square, shallow piece that measured 9–12 inches as a dish (58). Others called an odd shaped bowl a dish (59). Taylor Brothers and others joined three small shallow bowls and added a handle for a relish dish (60). A Libbey catalog pictured a large divided dish for hors d'oeuvre. Various dealers and collectors have incorrectly described these divided shapes as "strawberry" dishes (61).

LARGE JARS

During the Brilliant Period catalogs illustrated cracker jars that today get incorrectly referred to as "biscuit" jars, an English term, or "cooky" or "cookies" jars, a present-day name. The catalogs showed the cracker jars in four different shapes: all glass with a flat lid and finial (62); glass with a shallow silver lid (63); glass with a silver rim, lid, and handle (64); and glass that resembled a cigar jar but with a clear neck (65).

A number of older catalogs pictured a 5½-inch jar for cigarettes (66), an 8-inch one for cigars (67), and a 7-inch one for tobacco (68). Expect to find exceptions to these measurements among companies. The jars came with two types of lids: glass, and silver which needed enough depth for a sponge to keep the contents fresh (69). The craftsman ground the necks of the jars and lids for a tighter fit. "Humidor," a modern term, did not appear in the catalogs.

58. A 9-inch square dish with pinwheel as the dominant motif.

59. A crimp dish with a hobstar dominance.

60. Three hearts and a handle in another type of relish dish.

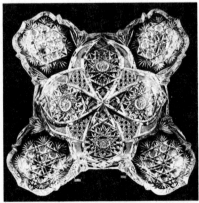

61. A square crimp dish that measures 14½ by 14½.

62. A cracker jar with lid and under plate.

63. A cracker jar with a silver lid.

64. A cracker jar with silver lid and handle.

65. A cracker jar that resembled a tobacco jar.

66. A cigarette jar in Marlboro by Dorflinger.

67. A cigar jar in Marlboro by Dorflinger.

68. A tobacco jar in Marlboro by Dor-flinger.

69. A tobacco jar with a deep silver lid.

TUBS

The catalogs described any containers for ice as a tub or bowl and not as a "bucket." The bowl usually added applied handles. Both the ice tub and bowl measured 6–8 inches in diameter. Normally companies made the tub in three general shapes: round with a liner and no handles (70), round with applied handles (71), and round with handles as an extension of the blank (72). The no-handled tub and a similar shape in a flower pot you often hear identified incorrectly as "champagne bucket." Originally, both of these shapes included metal liners, but we have seen only a few with liners intact.

For an additional fee, the catalogs offered a matching plate and drainer for the ice tub or bowl. The drainer consisted of a round piece of glass with small holes and sometimes supporting peg feet. Several companies produced specialized shapes in tubs. The Pairpoint Corporation and Libbey catalogs illustrated a tub with a silver rim and handles. You could easily confuse this shape with a cracker jar except the tub has no lid. A. L. Blackmer Company and Elmira fashioned an ice tub in the shape of a cradle (73).

We have heard the butter tub identified as a small ice tub. The butter tub measured approximately 5 inches in diameter, 2 inches deep, and came with or without a 7-inch plate (74). You could buy the butter tub with or without handles. A few catalogs offered the choice of a lid.

70. An ice tub in crosshatched diamonds and flat stars.

71. An ice tub or bowl with applied handles.

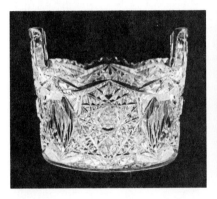

72. An ice tub with handles made by extending the blank.

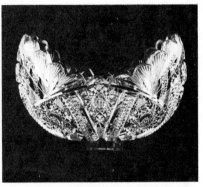

73. An ice tub in a cradle shape, Columbia pattern by Blackmer.

74. A butter tub with extended handles and plate.

FOOTED SHAPES

Companies put a foot on different shapes, but none described the foot as a "pedestal" or a "standard." A number of shapes in cut glass, such as comports and vases, included the foot as an integral part. From time to time the pattern maker added a foot as an extra to a piece that normally used none, raising its value. With most pieces the type of foot varied with the shape.

LOW FOOT

The low foot included a round base and a very short stem or none. Expect to find a low foot on a bowl (75), jug (76), carafe, mayonnaise, cake tray (77), loving cup (78), decanter, ice bowl, spooner (79), and celery (80). Several companies added a low foot to a sugar and cream, toothpick, and individual salts.

Comports also came with a low foot (81). The use of the present-day term "compote" appeared in some of the catalogs in the late Brilliant Period. A 1904 Libbey catalog used compote, but the next ones returned to comport. Small comports with handles and a low foot some have identified incorrectly as "footed nappies" (82), and the large oval ones (83) as "banana bowls on a pedestal." A few identified the covered comport pictured here as a "casserole" (84). Taylor Brothers added handles to a covered comport with a low foot and identified it as a compotier. The dictionary defines compotier as compote.

75. A bowl with a low foot in Berlyn by Quaker City.

76. A jug on a low foot.

77. A cake tray on a low foot.

78. A true loving cup with smooth rim and three handles on a low foot, in Libbey Imperial pattern.

79. A spooner on a low foot.

80. A celery on a low foot.

81. A scalloped hobstar on the low foot of a comport.

82. A two-handled comport on a low foot.

83. A large two-handled comport on a low foot.

84. A covered comport on a low foot in Delaware by Hawkes.

TALL FOOT

A tall foot with a round base and a long stem supported the bowl of a comport (85). Teardrops, notched flutes, and knobs decorated the comport stem. The star on the base of the foot blended with the design. You'll find the bowl of the comport deep or shallow, round or square. As in the celery, the craftsman cut the rim straight sawtooth, scalloped sawtooth, or rolled. Oddly enough, Clark called all comports footed bonbons, and Hawkes occasionally used this same term. Some frequently call one type of comport a "tazza vase" (86). The definition of tazza, an Italian term, is a "flat, ornamental cup, especially one supported on a high foot."

A few companies produced a one-piece comport punch bowl with a tall foot (87). We have seen only one divided comport (88). Several catalogs illustrated tall comports with handles. Along with a celery (89) and a cake tray (90), the catalogs pictured these popular shapes with a tall foot: spoon tray, puff box, violet vase, rose globe, sugar and cream.

85. A comport with a straight sawtooth rim on a tall foot. The stem has a teardrop and notched flutes while the base has a scalloped hobstar.

86. A comport frequently identified incorrectly as a "tazza vase."

88. A very rare divided comport on a tall foot.

87. A one-piece comport punch bowl.

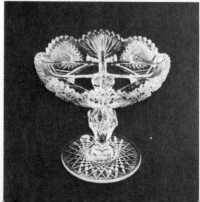

89. A celery on a tall foot.

90. A 12-inch cake tray on a tall foot that has a teardrop and scalloped base with a large hobstar.

PEG FOOT

At the mention of peg feet, you will immediately think of a fern. A fern or fern dish—not a "fernery"—usually came with smooth rim, in a round or hexagon shape, and with a liner (91). Ferns with sawtooth rims, such as Egginton cut, usually did not have liners (92). Companies made the fern with or without applied peg feet (93). Several companies added handles to the fern (94). The small fern measured 6 inches in diameter and the large one 8–9 inches. In limited numbers, the catalogs pictured peg feet on bonbons (95), bowls (96), baskets (97), vases, sugar and cream sets.

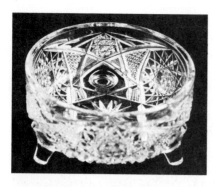

91. A fern with a smooth rim and peg feet.

92. A fern or fern holder with a straight sawtooth rim.

93. A fern without peg feet.

94. A fern with handles and four peg feet.

95. A bonbon with peg feet.   96. A rare bowl with peg feet.

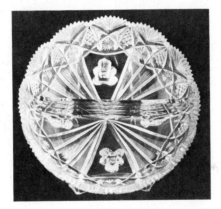

97. A basket with four peg feet.

SPECIALIZED FOOT

A specialized foot in the shape of a cone went on a two-part comport (98), a covered comport (99), and a sauce dish (100). A foot on a lamp consisted of a round hollow base and a stem similar to the shape of a vase (101). Hawkes created a unique two-piece bowl in which the round collar base contained four feet (102).

Most footed punch bowls rested on a round hollow base that varied in height (103) and in shape (104). J. Hoare & Company cut a comport punch bowl. The foot converted to a comport when turned upside down (105). Any foot complimented the shape of the punch bowl and definitely repeated the pattern.

98. A two-part comport with a cone foot.

99. A covered comport with a cone foot.

100. A sauce dish with a cone foot.

101. A foot on a lamp resembling a vase in Poppy by Pitkin & Brooks.

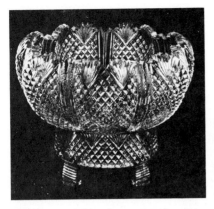

102. A collarlike foot on a bowl in Strawberry-Diamond and Fan by Hawkes.

103. A tall foot on a punch bowl.

104. A low foot on a punch bowl.

105. A punch bowl where the foot forms a comport.

MISTAKEN IDENTIFICATIONS

Reprints of old catalogs have done much to correct a number of wrong identifications of shapes. The dealer and the collector can do much to correct these errors and popularize the right name for the shape.

GUEST ROOM SET

"Tumble up," a borrowed name, did not appear in the catalogs, but these did: individual drinking water set, water bottle and tumbler, guest or sick room set (106). In one catalog Hawkes referred to this carafe and tumbler as an eye opener set. A late Dorflinger catalog pictured a night set consisting of a "tumbler, jug, safety match holder, candlestick and a one-drink decanter" set on a glass tray. Blackmer showed an unusual night cap set. A small bottle with a stopper fit securely into the neck of a carafe with a tumbler for a cover (107).

106. A guest room set in Marlboro by Dorflinger.

107. A night cap set with stoppered bottle that fits in neck of carafe.

CANDLESTICK

Candlestick included any shape that held a single candle (108). No catalog used the name "luster" or "chamberstick."

108. A pair of candlesticks signed by Hoare.

COLOGNE

Cologne described most scent bottles with a capacity of 3–18 ounces. Some wrongly identify the large size as a cordial decanter. Colognes came in a number of shapes: globe, squat, square, and round (109). The stopper might match the design (110), have a lapidary cut, or use silver. Companies also produced a tall perfume bottle (111), very small individual ones of an ounce or less in capacity, and atomizers. Vinaigrettes, pungents, or scent bottles have a straight or curved shape (112).

110. A cologne with a cut stopper that matches the bottle.

109. A globe-shaped cologne in Strawberry-Diamond and Fan.

111. A tall perfume bottle.

112. A scent bottle in cane with a silver top.

LADY'S FLASK

At an antiques show a dealer showed us a 4-inch, flat bottle with a sterling screwtop she called a "lay-down perfume bottle." The person in the next booth insisted on calling it a "muff bottle." An Unger Brothers catalog pictured it as a lady's flask (113). S. F. Meyers Company catalog illustrated such a flask with a removable silver cup that slipped over the base. The cup measured about one-third of the size of the bottle.

113. A lady's flask cut in Russian by Unger.

BOTTLES

Since bitter bottles have approximately the same top as barber bottles, this similarity has caused some confusion in identification (114). We have never found a barber bottle listed in any cut glass catalog. Robert Blake Powell, who collects barber supplies and has published two books on the subject, says that Theo. A. Kochs Company of Chicago and Koken of St. Louis sold most of the barber supplies. A Kochs catalog pictured two cut glass barber bottles (115). "These two barber supply companies," Powell suggested, "probably purchased the cut glass bottles on special order from a glass company."

114. A bitters bottle in an odd shape.

No. 228.
CUT GLASS STAND BOTTLE
Each $1.15

No. 209.
CLEAR GLASS STAND BOTTLE
Each .... 25c.

115. A page from Theo. A. Kochs Company catalog showing cut glass barber bottles.

CAKE TRAY

The catalogs illustrated the "cake stand" or "doughnut stand" as a cake tray. The cake tray measured 9–12 inches in diameter (116).

116. A footed cake tray sometimes referred to incorrectly as a "doughnut stand."

MUSHROOM SET

Two collectors showed us a "caviar set" (117). A Pairpoint catalog pictured a similar shape as a mushroom set. A Hawkes catalog listed a three-piece caviar set that included a small bowl with a clear glass liner and a large plate.

117. A mushroom set.

FLOWER HOLDER

We have never found any shape listed in a catalog as a "lady's spittoon." Both collectors and dealers have shown us a round deep shape—sometimes with a collar—they called a spittoon (118). Pairpoint called this same shape a flower holder. Another type of flower holder someone described as a "bishop's hat" (119). Flower holders came in other shapes with a glass or metal fitting for the inside. Several companies fitted the netting over the bowl (120). Pairpoint also pictured a flower canoe (121), sometimes incorrectly called a celery, and a tall flower basket (122).

118. A flower holder in Viscaria by Pairpoint, and not a spittoon.

119. A flower holder in Cambria by Egginton and not a "bishop's hat."

120. A flower holder intact with netting.

121. A flower canoe, sometimes mistaken for a celery, in Plaza pattern by Pitkin & Brooks.

122. A flower basket.

UNDER PLATES

Several collectors have identified a shape about 2 inches deep with a straight rim topped by a collar as a "wine coaster" (123). In various catalogs we have seen this shape under ice bowl or tub, jug, butter tub, mayonnaise, and covered butter or cheese and plate.

We purchased three "wine coasters" 5½ inches in diameter with straight rims (124). Imagine our surprise when we found them pictured in two catalogs, described for "butter balls, radishes, etc."

Various-sized plates have a slight indentation which indicated that they belonged with a two-piece set (125). Such plates went with a salad bowl, cracker jar, Roman punch cup, mustard, handled saucer, finger bowl, mayonnaise, or handleless sugar.

123. A plate that fits under various pieces in Grecian pattern by Hawkes.

124. A container for butter balls in Strawberry-Diamond and Fan, signed Hawkes.

125. Covered cheese and matching plate.

UNIDENTIFIED SHAPES

From time to time we have seen shapes for which we can find no catalog identification. We cannot dismiss the shapes lightly as "possibly made on special order" or "probably a presentation piece." A presentation piece usually has an inscription. Libbey and other companies did permit their workers to make whimseys from leftover metal, and these would not appear in a catalog. Sooner or later, an old catalog may provide the answer.

FISH TRAY?

The owner identified a tray 21½ by 6 inches for fish, but we found no similar shape in any catalog (126). Tuthill did decorate a tray 10 by 6 inches with a trout, but no one knows if he intended it for fish (127).

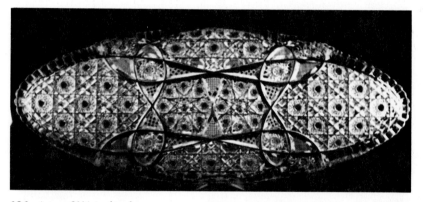

126. A tray 21¼ inches long.

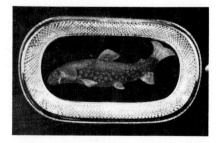

127. A tray cut by Tuthill.

PRESERVE DISH?

A small bowl in Clark's Galatea pattern fits perfectly into a sterling silver one. The dealer told us that she bought them together. Not even a Clark catalog illustrated such a piece (128).

128. A small bowl and silver holder in Galatea pattern by Clark.

TOUPEE STAND?

Two collections contained "toupee stands" signed Libbey (129). We talked with the dealer who identified this stand as "made on special order." He gave as his source the owner of the Parcel Post Cut Glass Company. If upended, it resembled a mayonnaise (130), but this would make the Libbey signature upside down.

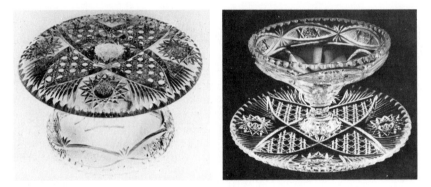

129 and 130. Two views of a piece identified as a toupee stand.

OIL AND VINEGAR?

A round 6-inch ball with a flattened knob on top contained an inside glass partition and two spouts (131). A worker might have made this as a whimsey.

We based these identifications of shapes on the most common usage, but you can always find special exceptions. To help you become more familiar with the most popular catalog names, the illustrations throughout this book will make identifications in terms most commonly used for different shapes.

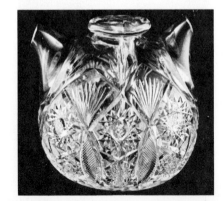

131. An interesting shape that might classify as a whimsey.

2

Matching Patterns

AT times a person will look at a cut glass bowl or vase and remark, "My mother had a piece exactly like that." Undoubtedly the mother did own a similar shape and possibly the same dominant motif, but probably not the identical pattern. *Motif* refers to a geometric or engraved figure on a piece of cut glass. To the amateur, all hobstar and pinwheel patterns look the same. By contrast, the dealer and collector look at the entire pattern and try to make a specific identification.

You can easily match a piece to such well-known geometric patterns as Parisian, Chrysanthemum, or Russian, but suppose you want to identify an unknown pattern? You tediously study patterns in antiques magazines, books, and old catalogs until every pattern looks alike.

You can simplify this search for identification by following a two-step analysis. A pattern consists of deep miter cuts that outline the design and of motifs that complete the pattern. First match the miter outline the rougher made and then match the motifs. A number of patterns contained a major and minor motif or two of equal importance. When you match both the miter outline and the motifs, you have identified the pattern. This method actually retraces the steps in cutting.

MITER OUTLINES

In a cutting shop the rougher marked, on a blank with a grease pencil or red liquid, the outline for the deep miter cuts. Experienced craftsmen frequently knew a pattern so well they could cut it without marking. This type of cutting did create slight differences in the pattern. A partly unpolished demonstration piece clearly illustrates how miters outline a pattern (132). In identifying patterns, we found ten basic miter outlines and various combinations.

132. A demonstration bowl, only partially polished, in Phoenix by Pairpoint that used a bar outline.

BARS

Double or multiple parallel miters formed bars that differed in width (133). The bars intersected in the center or else formed a square or triangle that accented a dominant motif. They may end in a point or straight line. Heavily cut patterns with highly decorated bars tended to blur or almost erase the miter outline (134).

133. A low bowl with a pattern formed by intersecting bars.

134. An ice cream tray with heavily decorated, intersecting bars that end in a point.

ROWS

In this outline, the miters separated horizontal rows of repetitive motifs as in cane on this clock (135). Sometimes a row might contain alternating motifs as in this bowl (136). The number of rows and the type of motifs depended on the size and shape of the piece. On the average, most designs contained two different rows repeated several times.

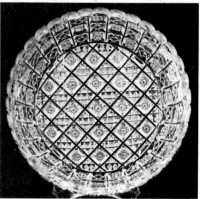

135. A clock cut in the row outline that formed cane.

136. A row outline in a low bowl that alternates hobstars with intersecting double miters.

BORDER AND MITER

One very popular outline consisted of a border, frequently of stars, and a series of perpendicular miters (137). These miters might vary in width and type of decoration. A few patterns used a double border (138). While the borders changed only slightly through the Brilliant Period, the decorations on the miters grew more ornate (139). Very simple miter patterns contained no border.

139. An 8-inch plate with ornate decorations on the miters but simple hobstar and double-fan border.

138. A jug with a double border and miter outline.

137. An oil lamp in border and miter outline, A. G. pattern by Clark.

STAR

The star often framed a hobstar center with a matching motif cut in the space above or between the points (140). Normally crosshatching filled the points of the star, but some used cane, crosscut diamonds, and other motifs. Craftsmen found several ways to vary the points of a star, such as cutting a double one (141) or alternating the motifs within the points (142).

140. A 9-inch plate in star outline with hobstars and fans.

141. A 10½-inch plate in a double star outline where hobstars alternate with elongated 8-point stars.

142. A 7-inch nappy bowl with ornate star points and triple pointed ovals.

GOTHIC ARCH

The Gothic arch possibly developed from Hawkes's very popular Chrysanthemum pattern. The curved miters met in a sharp point at the top, resembling a Gothic arch in architecture, and separated the dominant motif, such as a hobstar. This miter outline worked especially well with tall or large pieces (143). While some designs ornately decorated the arch, others kept it quite plain. The Gothic arch on a bowl, plate, or tray left the base open for a center motif or let the miters meet in a point that resembled the top of the arch (144).

143. A large vase in Gothic arch with hobstars.

144. A 9-inch low bowl where the Gothic arches meet at a point in the center.

PANELS

When roughing this outline, the craftsman normally radiated panels from a central point (145) except in a comport because of the application of the foot. While some panels measured the same length and width, others alternated a wide with a narrow one. Still other patterns graduated the width. The motifs within the panel might repeat the same ones, as in Hawkes's Panel pattern, or contain alternating ones (146).

145. A 10-inch plate with alternating panels of hobstars and crosshatched triangles.

146. A 12-inch tray with panels of differen widths and motifs.

SWIRLS

Swirls gave the panel a whirling or spinning effect. Possibly the credit for such a design should go to the appearance of Halley's Comet. Libbey (147) and Hoare cut the two best-known swirl patterns called Comet, but we have not found a verification of this name in a catalog, indicating possibly a descriptive one. The type of motifs within the swirls varied with the design. Some patterns alternated two designs of swirls (148), while others combined

147. A 7-inch plate signed Libbey and in "Comet," swirl outline.

148. A berry bowl with alternating swirls of cane and of hobstars and crosshatched triangles.

149. A 9-inch low bowl where cross-hatching and cane unite to form a swirl.

150. A berry bowl that uses three types of swirls in the outline.

two different swirls to make one unit (149). An ornate pattern used three repetitive swirls (150).

POINTED LOOPS

The pointed loops outline relied on curved miters that coiled around the minor motifs of the pattern. On a tray, bowl, or plate the loops might frame a hobstar center (151) or meet at a central point (152). One or a combination of motifs filled the pointed loops or ovals, depending on the brilliance of the pattern and the size of the piece. You might know the pointed oval by the descriptive term "vesica." The dictionary defines vesica as "a bladder, an oval aureole in pictural art, a pointed curved figure in architecture." Pointed oval seems a more appropriate term.

151. A 7-inch plate in the pointed loops outline and hobstars.

152. A pointed loops outline on a low bowl where points meet at the center.

CIRCLES

This outline differed from the pointed loops in that the circles or impressions of such framed the dominant rather than the minor motif (153). In a very brilliant piece, the circles intersected or overlapped (154).

153. Independent circles frame the flashed hobstar of this 14-inch tray in circle outline.

154. A 14-inch tray where circles intersect to provide more brilliant cutting.

DUAL MOTIFS

In a number of patterns, the miters left spaces for a single and a combination motif within a diamond (155) or pointed oval (156). The combination ranged from simple to complex with two to four motifs. It might function as either a major or minor motif in the pattern. The group, rather than the single motif, provides the best key to the identification of the pattern.

COMBINATIONS

As the demand for new patterns increased through the years, the pattern maker combined two miter outlines. He combined the circle with bars (157), the pointed loops with the circle (158), and the star with the Gothic arch (159). Combination outlines provided unlimited possibilities for patterns during the Brilliant Period.

Take the first step in matching a pattern by locating the miter outline and finding a duplicate in a catalog, magazine, or book. Do only one piece at a time to avoid confusion. Once you have matched the miter outline, next check the individual motifs.

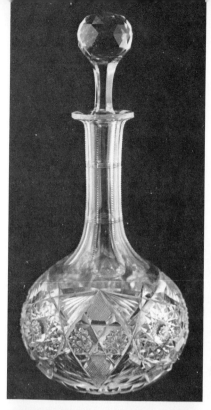

155. A decanter with hobstars and dual diamond motif of crosshatching and flat stars.

156. A 10-inch tray in dual motifs of hobstars and a combination of flat and 8-point stars in a pointed oval.

157. An 8-inch berry bowl that combines the circle and the bar outline.

158. A bonbon that combines the pointed loops with the circle.

159. An 8-inch nappy bowl with peg feet united the star and Gothic arch.

THE MOTIFS

You probably already know many of these motifs, but a review will reinforce your knowledge. In your identification allow for very slight differences in motifs as caused by different shapes.

LINES

You already know how the deep miters outlined the pattern. At the beginning of the Brilliant Period, the artisan cut the miters straight in simple designs (160). But soon the curved miter took over (161) and allowed for more complicated patterns and greater prismatic beauty. Notching on deep, parallel miters formed beading (162). Notching ranged from plain to elaborate (163).

Short, deep miters radiating from a focal point created fans (164). Fans consisted of 3, 5, 7, 9, or 11 prongs, the number increasing with the brilliance of the glass. The designer put fans between the prongs for flashing (165) or joined them with notching (166). In a few patterns the designer reversed the generally accepted direction of the fan (167).

Shallow miters created a number of motifs. Steps—horizontal miters—decorated the neck or foot of such pieces as comport, vase (168), lamp (169), foot of a punch bowl (170), cover for cheese or butter. Blaze or fringe, a motif frequently used by the English and Irish, consisted of shallow parallel lines that formed a border. By lengthening and shortening the lines, the pattern maker created a scalloped or pointed fringe (171). In the later Brilliant Period, these shallow lines formed a plume, fern, or feathering around the motif (172).

Minute perpendicular lines produced crosshatching, a motif that resembled a window screen (173). Crosshatching served as a repetitive minor motif encased in a square, triangle, diamond, or pointed oval (174). Modern and a few Canadian companies left the crosshatching unpolished and sometimes rough.

160. A six-inch plate cut with straight miters.

161. A 12-inch tray which uses curved miters.

162. Beading circles the pointed oval in this celery.

163. Simple notching of the miters on a vase.

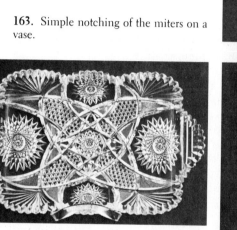

164. Eleven-pronged fans decorate the corners of this 8½- by 13½-inch tray.

165. A flashed fan on a footed jug.

166. Notched fans on a 7-inch plate in the star outline.

167. Reverse fans on an 8-inch berry bowl.

168. Step cut on the neck of a vase.

169. Step cutting on the foot of a lamp.

170. A punch bowl with steps cut on the foot.

171. Blaze on a vase.

172. A cheese and cracker dish with blaze or feathering on buzzstar and leaves.

173. Crosshatched diamonds on a 13-inch tray.

174. Crosshatched pointed ovals on a footed punch bowl.

DIAMONDS

American cutters borrowed the pointed diamond from the English and the Irish to use as a minor motif, such as a band or a decoration within a triangle (175). From this pointed diamond came a number of different adaptations. The cutter removed the sharp point from the diamond for the nailhead, so called because it resembled the top of a nail (176). Making two intersecting cuts across the top of the point created the crosscut diamond (177). All three of these diamond motifs often formed part of a combination.

In a relief diamond the artisan enlarged the pointed diamond and cut it with six or eight distinct facets (178). Some cutters left the diamond clear and fairly flat (179). Other patterns split the clear diamond with a short single miter or intersecting ones (180). The oval diamond, as previously mentioned, enclosed a group of motifs. The concave diamond also formed a group called honeycomb or St. Louis (181). This motif decorated the neck, foot, or handles of carafes, jugs, or lamps. As cutting grew more ornate, a hexagon replaced the four-sided diamond in the cluster.

The button in cane and hob in hobnail patterns also used the hexagon shape (182). Do not confuse cane with nailhead diamond. In cane two or three parallel lines separate the buttons, while the nailhead uses none.

175. Pointed diamonds decorate the corners of this square bonbon.

176. Nailheads fill the diamonds on this 10- by 11-inch tray.

178. A covered sugar bowl cut with a relief diamond.

177. A cracker jar cut in Strawberry-Diamond.

179. A two-handled low bowl with clear diamonds.

180. An 8-inch berry bowl where intersecting cuts divide the squares, signed by Libbey.

182. A 7½-inch plate in cane shows the hexagon shape.

181. A pepper sauce bottle with the neck cut in the St. Louis diamond.

STARS

In many patterns the artisan cut a star as the dominant motif. The type ranged from a single star to a complex rosette. The single star consisted of miters of equal length radiating from a focal center (183). Occasionally Hawkes and Dorflinger varied the length of the miters.

The pyramidal star turned the rays of a single star into an elongated, solid, triangular shape (184). The single and pyramidal star appeared mostly on the base or foot of an item, and, at times, as a dominant motif. A round concave center, heavy notching, and flashing converted a single star into a sunburst (185).

The pattern maker developed the raised star by reducing the number of miters and by cutting them wider and deeper (186). Heavy flashing changed this motif to a shooting star (187). Do not confuse the shooting star with the flashed star, which consisted of a special 8–10 point hobstar with fan accents (188). Outlining the single star with short, thin lines or blaze produced the feathered or blazed star. Libbey and Hawkes cut a special 5-point star used both as a major and minor motif.

The 8-point star formed the dominant motif in fairly simple patterns (189). The motif became more ornate by adding a single star to the clear center or crosshatching it. Some cutters filled the spaces around the points with crosshatching or single stars. In several patterns the 8-point star alternated with the hobstar.

The hobstar had a raised center like the hob on a man's boot (190). The number of points ranged from 8 to 64. The more points on the star, the more brilliant the piece. Some companies cut the hobstar in clusters (191) or as a border. Deep, minute cutting of the hobstar created the rosette (192).

The cutter stretched both the hobstar and the 8-point star to form an elongated one (193). As the cost of producing cut glass soared, companies substituted the flat star for the hobstar (194). Although it resembled the hobstar, the flat center reduced the cost of cutting. The flat star functioned as a dominant, dual, and minor motif.

183. A jug with the single star as the dominant motif.

184. A tray with a pyramidal star cut on either end.

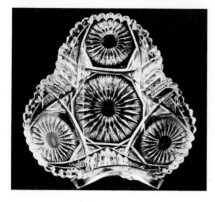

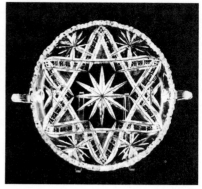

185. A bonbon with a sunburst as the dominant motif.

186. A 10½-inch low bowl with handles has a raised star as the dominant motif.

187. A 17- by 10-inch tray built the pattern around a shooting star.

188. An 8-inch nappy bowl with a flashed star as the dominant motif.

189. An 8-point star cut on a nappy.

190. Hobstars form the dominant motif on this very large punch bowl.

191. Clusters of hobstars fill the pointed loops on this 14-inch tray.

192. Six rosettes decorate this 7-inch plate.

194. Flat stars form the dominant motif on a small lamp.

193. A low bowl with an elongated hobstar and raised star in the center.

BUZZSAW

The buzzsaw motif became popular after 1900. It combined a raised hobstar center with straight miters and fans that projected a spinning buzzsaw. The number of fans and miters determined the type. In most patterns the buzz turned clockwise, but in a few it turned counterclockwise.

The pinwheel contained the most miters and fans (195). Because this motif required considerable space, you find it especially on large pieces. A few craftsmen cut ferns between the miters or added fans to the tips for more brilliance.

To cut labor cost, the buzzstar reduced the size, the number of miters, and fans in the pinwheel (196). The buzz, often with a flat center, had the least number of miters and fans (197). In later years the deletion of the fans left a stripped buzz. Today the buzz decorates much imported lead crystal. Apparently Hawkes never used the buzz motif as none appeared in the available catalogs.

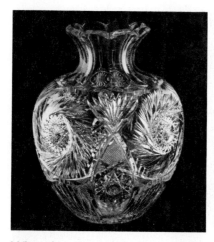

195. A large vase with the pinwheel motif.

196. A 7½-inch nappy bowl with a dominance of buzzstars.

197. A whiskey bottle with a buzz motif.

OTHER MOTIFS

The block motif soon disappeared as a pattern but occasionally functioned as a minor motif. It has become popular in recent years as a pattern on imported glass.

Flutes consisted of concave or flat panels. Several large companies, such as Hawkes, Libbey, and Dorflinger, cut flute patterns. Later this motif chiefly decorated the necks of carafes (198), the feet of comports, vases and lamps, and the lips of jugs (199). Half flutes resulted from placing a band around the long flutes or cutting only half of the motif (200). Old Bohemian glass used the half flutes consistently as a border. H.P. Sinclaire & Company revived the flute pattern during the late Brilliant Period.

An oval or concave circle took the name of thumbprint, punty, puntie, or bull's-eye (201). The English and the Irish used this motif frequently, but its popularity soon waned in the United States.

Late in the Brilliant Period, Libbey (202) and Meriden Cut Glass Company used a Roman or Greek key as a border. The Heart motif united the approximate shape of a heart with fans at the dip (545). The design probably originated with Pitkin & Brooks. The late William Wickson, a master cutter, told us that he created the motif while working for this company. Parsche and others kept the general shape but changed the interior design of the heart (203).

Compare the motifs with the matching miter outline. Once you have matched your piece to the illustration in a book, magazine, or catalog, you can go to work on another item. This method of matching a piece to a picture of a pattern anyone can easily learn.

198. Flutes on the neck of a carafe.

199. Flutes on the lip of a jug with shooting star and pinwheel.

200. Half flutes on a decanter with facet cut neck rings.

201. Punties alternate with deep miter cuts on this punch bowl.

202. A 9-inch berry bowl in Libbey's Greek Key pattern and with signature.

203. A heart motif filled with a cluster of hobstars in a fancy dish.

3

Identification by Catalog Name

MOST companies put a number or a date or both on their published catalogs. One person whose grandfather owned a cutting shop suggested that some companies numbered their issues rather than dated them so they appeared more current. Others, he pointed out, would use a number higher than they actually published to infer they produced a larger selection of cut glass.

The catalogs contained new patterns not previously advertised along with a few of the popular designs from previous issues. Each catalog headlined one or two patterns by illustrating them in all different shapes. Periodically some companies, such as Libbey and Hawkes, went back as far as ten years and reprinted the most popular patterns in a special edition. A few companies, Elmira for instance, numbered all patterns while Hawkes and Libbey named most designs but listed a few by number.

Names for cut glass patterns came from practically any source. Often the name described the pattern, such as Basket, Heart, or Flute. Feminine names—Doris, Isabella, Gladys—proved most popular. In fact, Libbey named the Florence pattern for his bride.

Several companies, such as Hawkes and Hoare, selected names that reflected their background: Queens, Kings, Princess, Regal, or Kohinoor. Clark showed an affinity for Spanish names: San Mateo, San Remo, or Rio Grande. Geography furnished such names as Phoenix, Virginia, and Cyprus. As companies produced more and more glass, they duplicated names. Several companies used Harvard, Yale, Brazilian, or Marquise. The same name often identified a different pattern with a few exceptions.

Louis Iorio worked as a designer for Empire Cut Glass Company. According to Bill Iorio, his son, those who created the patterns chose the name. "Occasionally management would name a pattern," he added, "but Pop named most of those he designed." Donald Parsche said his father designed and named the patterns cut in this shop. Miss Lucille Egginton told us her father created and named the patterns for his company. Charles Tuthill,

according to Wallace Turner, performed these same functions for the Tuthill
Cut Glass Company.

Regardless of the sources for names or those who chose them, a collector or
dealer always experiences satisfaction in identifying a piece of cut glass by the
catalog name. Knowing the characteristics of patterns cut by individual companies often can provide a valuable clue to identification.

WELL-KNOWN COMPANIES

Most factories or shops cut a general line of standard (204) as well as quality
cut glass (205). While both types employed the same motifs, the quality
patterns exhibited more flair for design, accuracy of cutting, unique shape,
and excellence in blank.

J. D. BERGEN COMPANY
Meriden, Connecticut, 1880–1922

The Bergen patterns ranged from simple to complex, but all show an
artistic flair for design. The company glorified the notch miter. A jug in
Premier combined the notched miter with punties on the neck and added a

204. A bell in a standard cutting.

205. A finger bowl in a quality cutting.

60

hobstar border (206). On a decanter in Marie notched miters intervened between the stars (207). In the same manner, deep cut miters separated the 8-point stars in Niles (208). Tasso combined the notched miter with a diamond and fan border (209). While no records authenticated that Bergen created the sunburst motif, the company developed it most artistically in Goldenrod by cutting hobstars as the center and notching and flashing the miters (210).

At the height of the Brilliant Period, Bergen revived some simple motifs of earlier years to create new patterns. Oregon alternated the punty with the elongated 8-point star (211). Half flutes formed the border for crosshatched bands and flat stars in Glenwood (212). In Emblem, an irregular star outline with crosshatched points revived the 8-point star (213).

The company embellished basic motifs to produce artistic creations. In Bermuda, four flashed fans united hobstars (214). Progress combined the pointed loops and circles outlines and accented the cutting with fans that met on a straight line (215). In Allyn, Bergen intersected step cutting and changed the hob center of the pinwheel (216). The catalogs showed patterns that placed stars between the miters of a buzzstar or added fans to the tips of hobstars. These unusual designs may help you identify unsigned Bergen glass.

206. A jug in Premier by Bergen, 1904–1905 catalog.

207. A decanter with neck rings and honeycomb cut on handle in Bergen's Marie, 1904–1905 catalog.

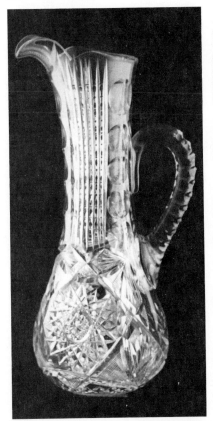

208. A nut dish in Niles by Bergen, 1907–1908 catalog.

209. A 12¾-inch tall wine bottle in Tasso by Bergen.

210. An 8-inch berry bowl in Goldenrod by Bergen, 1904–1905 catalog.

211. A syrup in Bergen's Oregon, 1904–1905 catalog.

212. A 14-inch, footed punch bowl in Glenwood by Bergen, 1904–1905 catalog and signed.

213. A bonbon in Emblem by Bergen, 1904–1905 catalog.

214. A 9-inch berry bowl in Bergen's Bermuda, 1904–1905 catalog.

215. A 12-inch punch bowl in Progress, the 1904–1905 Bergen catalog.

216. Allyn by Bergen, 1904–1905 catalog, in a jug.

T. B. CLARK & COMPANY
Honesdale, Pennsylvania, 1884–1930

Although Clark produced a wide selection of heavily cut patterns, certain individual or combination motifs offered excellent identification. No company did more to elevate the pinwheel and buzzstar to popularity. Oddly enough, most pinwheels turned clockwise for Clark except in Mont Clare where they spun counterclockwise. On the foot of this comport the pinwheel turned clockwise (217). The buzzstar on Clarendon whirled clockwise (218).

Clark created a number of patterns with a slightly raised, facet center or lapidary cut on both a major and minor motif. In Waldorf, a circle of hobstars surround the clear center (219). The outer edge of a hobstar circled the clear raised center in Orloff (220).

In a special combination of motifs, crosshatched triangles met at a point to provide space for a fan at the top. The motif at the base of the combination changed with the particular pattern. In San Gabriel (543) the base motif contained a hobstar center surrounded by pointed diamonds in a square. A hobstar formed the base motif for Mayflower (221) and Harvard (222).

Crosshatching decorated some of the earlier patterns. In Arbutus, crosshatching accented the 8-point star (223), and in Baker's Gothic crosshatched hexagons formed a background effect for the stars (224).

Many of Clark's patterns focused on the hobstar as a dominant motif. Jersey, a simple pattern, joined hobstars with fans and miters (225). Owl alternated the hobstar with the 8-point star in a combination diamond (226). Mercedes, a very ornate pattern, complimented hobstars with such minor motifs as crosshatching, small hobstars, reverse fans, and steps (227).

Bars outlined some of Clark's patterns. In Homer, bars with rounded loops left space for hobstars (228). Camelia combined pointed loops and bars with flat stars (229).

Ferns or plumes dominated patterns. As early as 1905, Clark designed Fernhurst where ferns accented a shooting star (230). The company created a few notched miter patterns, as in A. G. (137). More often the notched miter functioned as a minor motif. With the exception of these characteristics, the large number of Clark's diverse patterns makes identification of cut glass most challenging.

217. Footed bonbon in Mont Clare by Clark, 1905 catalog.

218. The Clarendon pattern by Clark from 1908 catalog.

219. A 12-inch tray in Clark's Waldorf, 1901 catalog.

220. A footed punch bowl in Orloff by Clark, signed and pictured in 1905 catalog.

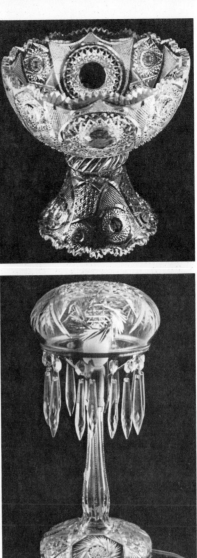

221. A decanter in Mayflower by Clark, 1905 catalog.

223. A footed 10-inch tray in Arbutus by Clark, 1896 catalog.

222. A small lamp in Harvard by Clark, 1904 and undated catalog.

224. A rectangular 14-inch tray in Baker's Gothic by Clark.

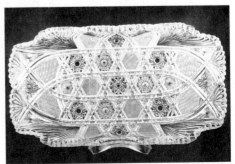

225. A butterette in Clark's Jersey, 1908 catalog.

226. A comport which Clark called a footed bonbon in Owl, 1908 catalog.

227. Mercedes by Clark, signed and in 1901 catalog, in a jug.

228. Low bowl signed Clark and in 1905 catalog as Homer pattern.

229. A low bowl in Camelia, signed Clark, undated catalog.

230. A tumbler in Clark's Fernhurst, 1905 catalog.

C. DORFLINGER & SONS
Brooklyn, New York, 1852–1863
White Mills, Pennsylvania, 1865–1964

Simplicity dominated many of Dorflinger's patterns. An early catalog illustrated patterns in Hob Diamond (231) and Hob and Lace (232). The company cut a Russian and a Russian-type design. The pattern with a small single star and a hobstar on the button the company called Russian (233). The design with a large single star and hobstar on a very small button, the catalog listed as Brilliante (234). The center hobstar of Covina added the only elaborate motif to a simple pattern of hobstars and triple miters (235).

Several of Dorflinger's row outlines contained a crosshatched diamond. Pattern #28 consisted of alternating crosshatched and crosscut diamonds (236). In Royal, double fans accented a square formed with crosshatched diamonds and single stars (237).

Fans accented several patterns. Essex, a simple one, used hobstars and large reverse fans (238). Parisian alternated regular and reverse fans with crosshatched diamonds. Parisian introduced the curved miter and also the Brooklyn Star. On trays and bowls a flashed star the craftsmen called the Brooklyn Star occupied the center of the pattern (239). Possibly the star developed at the Brooklyn factory.

231. Hob Diamond by Dorflinger in a decanter, catalog 51.

232. Matching colognes in Dorflinger's Hob and Lace, catalog 51.

233. A rose globe in Russian by Dorflinger, catalog 51.

234. A celery in Brilliante by Dorflinger, catalog 51.

235. A nappy in Covina by Dorflinger, catalog 51.

236. A 9-inch berry bowl in pattern #28 by Dorflinger, catalog 51.

237. A cologne in Dorflinger's Royal, identified from magazine advertisement.

238. A cologne in Essex by Dorflinger, *Antiques Magazine*.

239. A square plate in Parisian with the Brooklyn star by Dorflinger, catalog 51.

Curved miters and 8-point stars appeared in other patterns. In Sultana, the curved miters framed an 8-point star that alternated with a single one (240). Marlboro consisted of 8-point stars, fans, and intersecting fans with cross-hatched diamonds (106).

During the height of the Brilliant Period, Dorflinger added more ornate motifs to the simple ones of the past. Anona highlighted hobstars and ferns but retained the old 8-point stars and pointed diamonds (241). The addition of more motifs in later years changed the charming simplicity of the Dorflinger style of cutting.

240. A low bowl in Sultana by Dorflinger, catalog 51.

241. Footed punch bowl in Anona by Dorflinger, catalog 1881–1921.

O. F. EGGINTON COMPANY
Corning, New York, 1899–1920

Egginton's patterns suggested a rhythmic movement created by the miter cuts. A number of patterns displayed a characteristic combination of double curved miters that intersected to form a crosshatched diamond. This combination motif appeared either at the rim or near the base of the piece in such patterns as Creswick (842), and some of Marquise (242).

Occasionally, Marquise gets mistaken for Lotus because of the fan motif. The fans in Marquise contained a long center prong and shorter side ones. In Dryden, the intersecting miters appeared below or above the hobstar border, depending on the location of the notched miters (243). Orient also topped the major motif with this same combination (244). Cambria reversed the combination, placing the crosshatched diamond above the intersecting miters (119). Castilian elongated the crosshatched diamond (245).

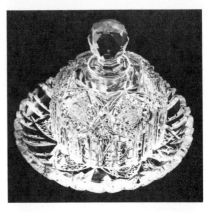

242. A comport in Marquise by Egginton, in catalog.

243. Butter dish in Dryden by Egginton, in catalog.

244. A cream to a set in Orient by Egginton, identified in catalog.

245. A nappy in Castilian by Egginton, in catalog.

246. An ice cream tray in Sherwood by Egginton, identified by catalog.

247. A sugar to a set in Tokio by Egginton, in catalog.

248. A 7-inch plate in Prism by Egginton, pictured in catalog.

249. A 14-inch punch bowl in Arabian by Egginton, illustration in catalog.

In some patterns, Egginton used space to emphasize the major motifs. In Sherwood, punties framed hobstars between the swirl center that provided the rhythm (246). Space accented the single sunburst motif in Tokio (247). An 8-point star border and alternating wide and narrow miters formed Prism (248). Perhaps the Arabian pattern best illustrated the rhythmic and detailed cutting so characteristic of Egginton (249).

EMPIRE CUT GLASS COMPANY
Flemington, New Jersey, 1904–1925

Louis Iorio created patterns with strong miter outlines for this company (250). Bill Iorio identified the following patterns from pieces in his private collection. In a number of patterns Iorio favored the bar outline. Notched miters formed the bars for Kremlin (251). Hobstars decorated the bars in Isabella, a heavily cut pattern (252).

The star outline offered an opportunity for variety in the simple pattern of Typhoon (253) and the more complicated one of Dupont (254). In both, crosshatching filled the points of the star. In Manhattan, Iorio decorated the star with a diamond of cane and triangles of crosshatching (255). This illustration in the catalogs pictured a hobstar rather than a reverse pinwheel in the center. Bill Iorio explained that they made such changes at the buyer's request.

Iorio also cut other miter outlines. Notched miters and border highlighted several patterns, such as Waldorf (256). A chain of flat stars separated the notched miters, but hobstars formed the double borders. Intersecting pointed ovals joined the alternating motifs of single stars and crosscut diamonds in pattern #11-136 (257). In Berkshire, double flat stars framed the deeply cut hobstar (258). For the more ornate patterns, Iorio turned to the pointed loops outline as seen in Iorio Special (259). In conclusion, strong miter outlines provide the key to identifying Empire patterns.

250. The late Louis Iorio working on a piece of glass.

251. An 8-inch crimp bowl in Kremlin, 1906 Empire catalog.

252. An 8-inch bowl in Isabella, 1910 Empire catalog.

253. An 8-inch berry bowl in Typhoon, 1910 Empire catalog.

254. An 8-inch berry bowl in Dupont, 1906 Empire catalog.

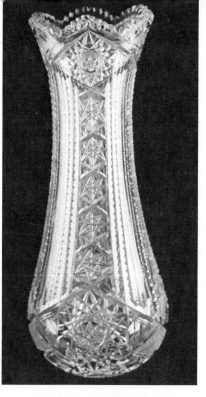

255. An 8-inch berry bowl in Manhattan, 1910 Empire catalog.

256. A vase in Waldorf, 1906 Empire catalog.

258. A 9-inch plate in Berkshire, 1910 Empire catalog.

259. A 9-inch bowl in Iorio Special, 1906 Empire catalog.

257. A decanter in #11-136 1906 Empire catalog.

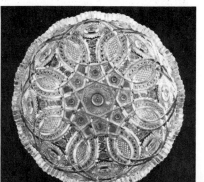

H. C. FRY GLASS COMPANY
Rochester, Pennsylvania, 1867–1934

Fry's cut glass suggested both an innovator and a practical businessman. He liked to experiment in glass formula, shapes, and patterns. His best blanks, sought by many cutting shops, contained a very high lead content. In shapes, for example, he created a two-lip cream in pattern 233½ (260 and 261).

The company also excelled in eye-catching designs, as in Frederick, that highlighted exotic fans and flashed stars (262). King George consisted of decorative squares (263). Chicago used intersecting bars of cane for the dominant motif and bars of hobstars for the miter outline (264). These designs seemed to express Fry's flair for living.

As a practical businessman, Colonel Fry saw the need for standard patterns for the average buyer as well as exotic ones for the carriage trade. Several companies cut the style of pattern seen in #104 (265). Hobstars dominated Sciota (266).

When engraving grew more popular, Fry added it to geometric designs, such as Vanity (267). When the cost of producing cut glass soared, he introduced the cheaper figured blank. The blower used a mold to shape the blank. The walls of the mold contained part of the pattern.

One difficulty in identifying unsigned Fry cut glass developed because of his association with two other companies, the Rochester Tumbler Company that numbered the patterns and the Empire Cut Glass Company. The same pattern might appear in catalogs for all three. Orient, a pinwheel design, appeared in both the Fry and Empire catalogs (268).

260. Sugar and cream in pattern #233½, signed Fry, in catalog.

261. A pattern view of the sugar in #233½.

262. A 12-inch tray in Frederick and signed Fry, pictured in catalog.

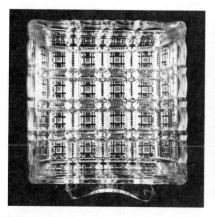

263. A bonbon signed Fry in King George pattern, illustration in catalog.

264. A 9-inch dish in Chicago by Fry, in catalog.

265. A plate in pattern #104, *Glass & Crockery Journal* advertisement, by Fry.

266. A 14-inch tray in Sciota, signed Fry and in catalog.

267. A nappy in Fry's Vanity, shown in catalog.

268. A jug signed Fry, named Orient in both Empire and Fry catalogs.

T. G. HAWKES & COMPANY
Corning, New York, 1880–1962

At the Paris Exposition in 1889, Hawkes achieved considerable recognition for American cut glass when he won the Grand Prix. At this Exposition he exhibited such patterns as Chrysanthemum (494), Grecian (123), and Venetian (269). His training as an engineer possibly influenced the precision seen in many of his patterns.

Although every company cut the Strawberry-Diamond and Fan pattern, only Hawkes seems to have signed it. These pieces show outstanding workmanship (270). He frequently created other designs with the strawberry diamond motif. In Astor, Hawkes combined the strawberry diamond with triangles of crosshatching and fans (271). Regina consisted of the strawberry diamond and a border of elongated hobstars (272).

Hawkes designed the Russian pattern for the Russian Embassy in the United States. Later the American Embassy in Russia and the White House selected this pattern for the state dinner set. A person whose grandfather worked for Corning Glass Company showed us a bowl in the Russian pattern with the family initials in the space where the seal of the United States appeared (273).

As with the Strawberry-Diamond and Fan pattern, the company created new designs by combining other motifs with the Russian. Alexander placed a blazed border around the Russian cut with a hobstar on the button (274). A band of Russian and deep miter cuts formed the alternating swirls in Russian

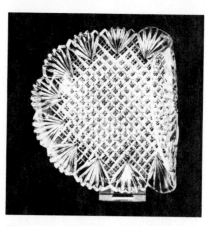

269. A 7-inch plate signed Hawkes in Venetian.

270. A 5-inch bonbon signed Hawkes in Strawberry-Diamond and Fan.

271. A 7-inch plate in Astor, signed Hawkes, in catalog.

272. A vase signed Hawkes in catalog as Regina.

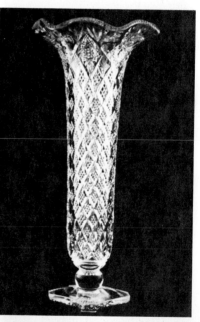

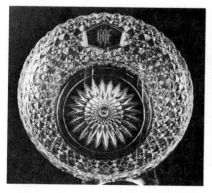

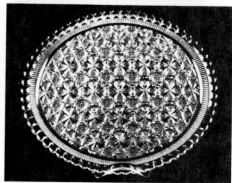

273. A 9-inch berry bowl in Russian with family initials placed where seal of United States went.

274. An oval tray in Alexander signed Hawkes and illustrated in catalog.

and Pillars (275). A scroll-like border and Russian with a single star on the button created Persian and Pillars (276).

Several patterns showed the dominance of rows in both simple and complex designs. Thistle contained a raised star center and four types of rows: large pointed diamond, small diamond, leaf, and beading (277). In Alberta, a clear row separated two of strawberry diamond, and blaze formed the border (278). Paul Revere broke the rows of thumbprint and crosshatching with a single star in a circle (279). A row of short notched miters separated those of hobstars in Constance (280).

Hawkes found various ways to emphasize the 8-point star. Leaf contained fans and 8-point stars (281). In Mars, crosscut diamonds alternated with the 8-point star (282). Crosscut diamonds framed the 8-point star in Cecil (283). Cambridge alternated strawberry diamonds and 8-point stars (284).

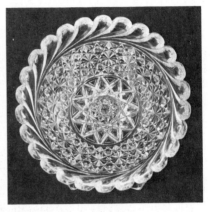

276. A bowl in Persian and Pillars by Hawkes illustrated in catalog.

275. Vase in Russian and Pillars and illustrated in Hawkes catalog.

278. A footed low bowl in Alberta by Hawkes, in catalog.

277. A bowl in Thistle by Hawkes located in catalog.

280. A fern dish signed Hawkes and named Constance in catalog.

279. A plate in Paul Revere by Hawkes, in catalog.

281. An individual butter in Leaf by Hawkes, shown in catalog.

282. A 14-inch ice cream tray in Mars by Hawkes according to a catalog.

284. A 7-inch plate in Cambridge located in Hawkes catalog.

283. A sugar to a cream in Cecil, signed Hawkes and shown in catalog.

Even at the height of the Brilliant Period, Hawkes continued to cut the 8-point star. In Canton, this star formed the border for the miters (285). Pointed ovals linked this star in Yeddo (286). Oakland elongated one point of this star to form the center (287). Intersecting miters framed the 8-point star in Kaiser (288). Alpine united elongated 8-point stars with three short miter cuts (289).

Fans frequently connected the dominant motifs. In Yale, simple fans linked the 8-point star (290). Flashed fans framed the flat stars in Harvard (291). Double fans joined the 8-point stars in Cyprus (292) and the single stars in New Princess (293). Palermo depended on double flashed fans to connect the hobstars (294).

In a number of patterns, Hawkes used two types of stars. Holland gave equal importance to the 8-point star and the hobstar (295). Minton contained the hobstar and the shooting star (296).

The hobstar did serve as the dominant motif in several patterns. In Keuka, hobstars completed the pointed loops outline (297). Pattern #60 used a decorative, pointed-loops outline with hobstars and shooting stars (298). Large hobstars formed the Dorcas pattern (299). Pairs of hobstars decorated a crimped bowl in pattern #1189 (300).

285. A saucer in Canton by Hawkes, seen in catalog.

286. A carafe signed Hawkes and illustrated in catalog as Yeddo.

287. A butter in Oakland pictured in Hawkes catalog.

288. A puff box with original puff that has silver knob, identified as Kaiser in Hawkes catalog.

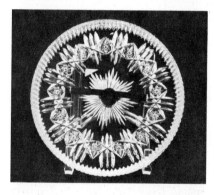

289. A nappy in Alpine, signed Hawkes and illustrated in catalog.

290. An oil in Yale, shown in Hawkes catalog.

291. An oil in Harvard, illustration in Hawkes catalog.

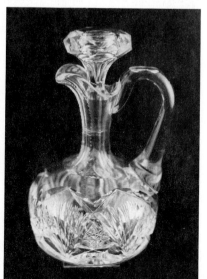

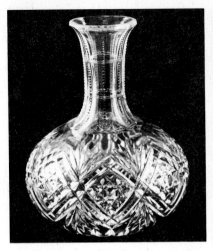

292. A carafe in Cyprus, signed Hawkes and in catalog.

293. A whiskey decanter or jug in New Princess, identified by Hawkes catalog.

294. A Fern in Palermo shown in Hawkes catalog.

295. A 10-inch plate in Holland with double Hawkes signature and pictured in catalog.

296. A handled bonbon in Minton, shown in Hawkes catalog.

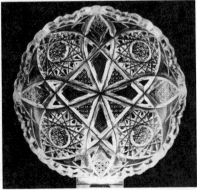

297. A nappy in Keuka, illustrated in Hawkes catalog.

298. A square bowl in pattern #60, signed Hawkes and in a catalog.

299. A sugar and cream on a foot found in Hawkes catalog as Dorcas.

300. A 9-inch crimp bowl in pattern #1189, signed Hawkes and in catalog.

Several patterns by Hawkes used clear areas in the form of punties, split diamonds, or wide miter cuts to accent the hobstars. Punties accented the stars in Princess, Queens (509), and Kings (510). Navarre combined the clear split diamond with hobstars and fans (301).

Hawkes highly developed the panels in several patterns. Hobstars top the panel outline in Napoleon (302). Fans and hobstars formed the panels in pattern #1286 (303). Lorraine alternated a large hobstar with a panel of hobstars (304). Panels of hobstars alternated with small hobstars and cross-hatched diamonds to form Valencia (305).

The company also cut swirl outlines, closely related to the panel designs. Pattern #1285 used two swirls: one of hobstars and the other of notched miters (306).

Patterns with notched miters showed the same degree of excellence as those of Bergen. Well-known patterns of this type include Brunswick (511) and Marquis (512). In Teutonic, the notched miters alternated with a panel of elongated hobstars (307). Atlantic separated a combination motif of flat stars and crosshatching with pointed ovals of notched miters (308).

As engraving grew in popularity, Hawkes produced scenes framed with geometric borders. Deer depicted two deer leaping across a clearing in a wooded area (309). Lake Lamoka gave a scenic view of a lake (310).

302. A 7½-inch plate in Napoleon, signed Hawkes and in catalog.

301. A vase in Navarre, signed and in Hawkes catalog.

303. Oval bowl in pattern #1286 pictured in Hawkes catalog.

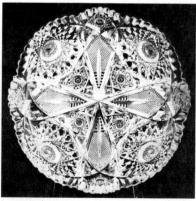

304. A comport signed Hawkes in Lorraine, illustrated in catalog.

305. An 8-inch berry bowl in Valencia identified by Hawkes catalog.

306. A crimp dish signed, in pattern #1284, Hawkes catalog.

307. A toothbrush bottle signed Hawkes in Teutonic as shown in catalog.

308. A 9-inch bowl in Atlantic, in Hawkes catalog.

309. A rectangular tray in Deer, illustrated in Hawkes catalog.

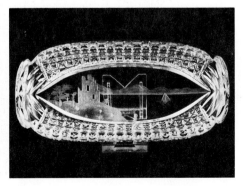

310. A 7½-inch relish or pickle dish in Lake Lamoka, pictured in Hawkes catalog.

J. HOARE & COMPANY
Brooklyn and Corning, New York, 1853–1920

Detailed cutting characterized the patterns of Hoare. He achieved this in several ways, such as individualizing well-known patterns. He divided the Russian pattern into panels with notched miters in pattern #5336 (311). The Gotham pattern varied a row of crosshatched buttons with one of hobstars (312). Pebble, a Corinthian type pattern, changed the center motif, enlarged the hobstars, and cut minute cane rather than the crosscut diamond (313).

Hoare changed simple patterns by adding more details. In Signora, he cut a double Gothic arch around the hobstars and added fans (314). A diamond that combined crosshatching and short miters linked the large and small hobstars in Eleanor, a Gothic arch outline (315).

Hoare frequently combined two miter outlines to provide more detailed cutting. Marquise united the Gothic arch with the star outline and added a hobstar border (316). Meteor framed intersecting bands of cane in the center with bars of hobstars (317). Steuben overlapped intersecting bars with a star outline (318). Hobstars completed the combination pattern of star and Gothic arch in Carolyn (319).

In a number of simple designs, Hoare outlined several hobstar patterns with crosshatched or feathered bars. While the patterns look the same, you can find slight differences. The bars in Florence started and ended with the hobstars (320). The Acme pattern extended the crosshatched bars to the rim of the piece (321). The bars in Venice stopped short of the rim and used either crosshatched or feathered cutting (322).

The company produced several notched miter patterns, well known among collectors and dealers. These patterns include Hindoo, Pluto, and Haydn which differ mainly in the type of border.

Halley's Comet certainly influenced Hoare. In Croesus, swirled miters formed a border for a band in diamonds of cane and double fans (323). Flashed fans swirled around the hobstars in Comet (324). Wheat alternated Russian with a leafy motif (325). Crystal City combined a caned swirl with circles and a flashed star in the center (326).

Hoare probably developed this talent for detail in patterns by studying those of other companies. We have seen his scrapbook, similar in size to large, leather-bound volumes found in tax offices (327). It included illustrations he had cut from his own catalogs and those of other companies. He arranged all of the "cutouts" alphabetically, such as bowls, carafes, and trays. He pasted the illustrations from his catalogs on the left hand page and those from other companies on the right.

Unfortunately, he gave these no identification as to company or pattern. In the center of the volume, he pasted entire sheets from one of his own catalogs. One page showed large trays (328) while another focused on sugar and cream sets (329). Vases dominated another page (330).

With very few exceptions these characteristics of cut glass by Hoare should help you recognize unsigned items.

311. A 14-inch bowl in pattern #5336, shown in Hoare catalog.

312. A celery in Gotham by Hoare.

313. An 8-inch square bowl in Pebble by Hoare, found in catalog.

314. A jug in Signora, illustrated in Hoare catalog.

315. An oil lamp in Hoare's Eleanor, identified by catalog.

316. An 11-inch square bowl, signed Hoare, in Marquise, pictured in 1911 catalog.

317. A 17-inch ice cream tray in Meteor by Hoare, shown in catalog.

318. A comport signed Hoare in Steuben, 1911 catalog.

319. A 12-inch tray in Carolyn by Hoare, 1911 catalog.

320. A nappy in Florence, signed Hoare, in 1911 catalog.

321. A six-inch plate in Acme, signed Hoare, 1911 catalog.

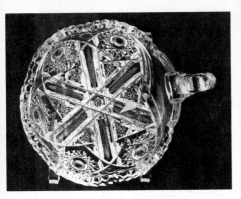

322. A handled nappy in Venice, signed Hoare and in 1911 catalog.

323. A vase in Croesus by Hoare, in catalog.

324. A jug in Comet by Hoare.

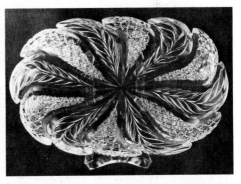

325. A 13½-inch ice cream tray in Wheat by Hoare, found in catalog.

326. A 9-inch bowl in Crystal City, pictured in Hoare catalog.

327. The scrapbook of Hoare.

328. Pages from scrapbook that illustrate ice cream trays.

329. Pages from Hoare scrapbook that picture sugar and cream sets.

330. Pages from Hoare scrapbook that show vases.

LIBBEY GLASS COMPANY
Toledo, Ohio, 1880–1924

Elaborate describes the patterns by Libbey. Although simple motifs formed the patterns, few pieces contained uncut surface. A number of patterns divided the cutting in rows. Royal consisted of a row of crosshatched and crosscut diamonds and one of clear split diamonds (331). Three rows made up the Victoria pattern: fans, 8-point stars, and fans (332). One of the most heavily cut patterns, Florence, included rows of fans, a combination of crosshatched diamonds, single stars, and hobstars (333).

Libbey cut a number of patterns that utilized notched miters. Prism consisted of fancy notched miters and a band of cane (334). Fans and elongated 8-point stars formed a border for notched miters in pattern #83 (335).

Bar outlines provided Libbey an opportunity for both simple and complex patterns. Elmore intersected notched bars to frame flat stars (336). Regis, a 1920 pattern, used two types of intersecting bars, one of notched miters and the other of hobstars (337). In Stratford, two hobstars and a single star decorated the bars (338). Bars of nailhead diamonds formed squares for hobstars in Isabella (339). Libbey cut a similar pattern, #205, in 1909, with intersecting pointed bars (340). Pointed bars of hobstars and crosshatched diamonds characterized Leota (341). Diagonal bars bordered hobstars in pattern #221 (342). Colonna contained pointed bars of hobstars and flat stars (343).

332. An ice cream tray in Victoria by Libbey, 1893 catalog.

333. A 10-inch bowl in Florence by Libbey, 1896 catalog.

331. A champagne in Royal by Libbey, 1893 catalog.

335. A jug in pattern #83, 1908 Libbey catalog.

334. A jug in Libbey's Prism, 1898 catalog.

336. A comport in Elmore, signed by Libbey and in 1904 catalog.

337. An 8-inch pickle tray signed Libbey in Regis, 1920 catalog.

338. An ice cream tray in Libbey's Stratford, 1893 catalog.

339. An 8-inch bowl in Isabella, 1893 Libbey catalog.

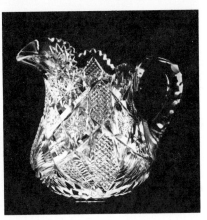

340. Pattern #205 signed Libbey in a jug, 1909 catalog.

341. A 10-inch tray signed Libbey in Leota pattern according to 1904 catalog.

343. A 7-inch plate in Libbey's Colonna, 1905 catalog.

342. A decanter signed Libbey in pattern #221, 1909 catalog.

Several Libbey patterns joined hobstars with a combination of motifs. In Neola, four flashed fans and a small hobstar formed the combination (344). For Senora notched steps in a pointed oval linked the hobstars (345). Triple fans and four-part squares united the hobstars in pattern #100 (346). Intersecting pointed ovals topped by a fan joined the hobstars in Sultana (347). A combination motif of cane unified the hobstars in Ozella (348). Waverly used a combination motif of reverse fans, 5-point stars and fans between the hobstars (349). Triangles of crosshatching and fans completed a hobstar pattern in #64 (350).

Panels highlighted three patterns. Columns of elongated stars characterized pattern #31 (351). A pattern described as "snowflake" but cataloged as #300 contained panels of crosscut diamonds (352). Circles intersected the panels. Two types of panels marked the Wedgmere pattern: one of hobstars and crosshatching and another of three types of decorated miters (353).

344. A 12-inch tray in Neola, signed Libbey and in 1904 catalog.

345. A pair of toasting cups in Senora by Libbey, 1904 catalog.

346. A jug signed Libbey in pattern #100, 1908 catalog.

347. An advertising plate in Sultana by Libbey, 1900–1910 catalog.

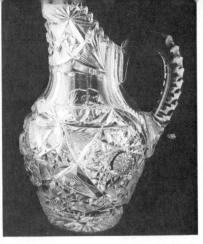

348. A 12-inch tray in Ozella by Libbey, 1908 catalog.

349. A jug in Waverly, a shape used only by Libbey, signed and in 1900–1910 catalog.

350. A nappy signed Libbey in pattern #64, 1908 catalog.

352. A 10-inch plate in pattern #300 by Libbey.

351. A vase in pattern #31 by Libbey, 1904 catalog.

353. A 17½-inch tray in Wedgmere, 1893 Libbey catalog.

Libbey developed totally cut patterns from any miter outline. A combination diamond of nailhead, crosshatching and hobstar broke the monotony of the cane motif in Avon (354). Hobstars enclosed in diamonds intercepted the intersecting steps in pattern #1903 (355).

Several elaborate patterns developed from the Gothic arch. That of Imperial provided space for alternating motifs of cane and hobstar diamonds (356); Aztec closed the Gothic arches and filled the spaces between with a fan-shaped motif of miters cut in beading and in small hobstar (357). Kenmore united the Gothic arch with the pointed loops outline (358).

Libbey cut very ornate patterns in the pointed loops outline. Columbia placed a pointed oval similar to a Gothic arch around the loops and added hobstars (359). An oval loop united clusters of hobstars in Marcella (360). Kensington contained hobstars between and within the pointed loops (361). Pointed loops framed a hobstar and a shooting star between large hobstars in pattern #125 (362).

Toward the end of the Brilliant Period Libbey simplified its cutting. Pattern #207 depicted a leafy cutting with a star (363). Leafy cutting with hobstars also characterized pattern #47 (364). A sparsely cut hobstar and double single stars comprised Melrose (365). Blazed buds and hobstars made up pattern #411 (366).

In its 1908 catalog, Libbey did more numbering of patterns. Numbering, however, did not affect the ornate cutting. In elaborate designs Libbey took an early lead and continued into the 1920s, when the company gradually turned to other type of glass.

354. An oval fruit bowl in Avon by Libbey, 1895.

355. A carafe and matching tumblers in pattern #1903 by Libbey, identified by magazine advertisement.

356. A celery in Imperial by Libbey, 1896 catalog.

357. A low 10-inch bowl signed Libbey in Aztec, 1900–1910 catalog.

358. An 8-inch berry bowl in Kenmore, signed Libbey, 1908 catalog.

359. An orange bowl in Columbia by Libbey, 1893 catalog.

360. A low 10-inch bowl in Marcella by Libbey, 1896 catalog.

361. A 12-inch tray in Kensington, signed Libbey, 1900–1910 catalog.

362. An 8-inch bowl signed Libbey in pattern #125, 1908 catalog.

363. A tumbler in pattern #207, signed Libbey, 1909 catalog.

364. A tumbler in pattern #47, signed Libbey, 1908 catalog.

365. A jug in Melrose signed Libbey, 1908 catalog.

366. A jug in pattern #411 by Libbey.

MT. WASHINGTON GLASS WORKS
New Bedford, Massachusetts, 1837–1894

PAIRPOINT CORPORATION
New Bedford, Massachusetts, 1880–?

Mt. Washington organized the Pairpoint Corporation in 1880 to manufacture useful and ornamental household goods in silver. In 1894, the Pairpoint Corporation took over Mt. Washington Glass Works. Little change appeared in the type of patterns. The two companies created some very interesting shapes and footed pieces in glass, such as footed spooners and celeries. Pairpoint also excelled in flower holders and center vases. Mt. Washington created a Russian pattern by adding deep cut, clear miters to break the overall pattern into panels (367).

A number of patterns used fan accents. In Wheeler, fans accented the rows of crosscut and crosshatched diamonds (368). Double fans emphasized the combination diamond motif in Magnolia (369). In Ucatena, double fans united a large hobstar (370). Reverse fans added the distinctive touch to Milano (371).

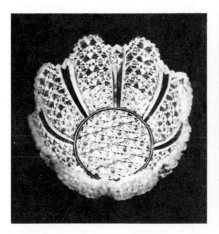

367. An 8-inch bowl in Russian by Mt. Washington, shown in catalog.

368. A sugar sifter in Wheeler by Mt. Washington, illustrated in catalog.

369. An 8-inch bowl in Magnolia by Mt. Washington, identified by catalog.

370. A flower holder in Ucatena pictured in Pairpoint catalog.

371. A crimp bowl in Milano, Pairpoint catalog.

Thin miters, sometimes notched, gave an individual touch to a number of Pairpoint patterns. Saratoga used notched miters and plain fans between large hobstars (372). Thin intersecting miters accented the star outline in Salem (373). This same type of miter formed the unique star that combined with the Gothic arches of cane for Silver Leaf (374).

Along with other companies, Pairpoint featured a hobstar as the major motif. In Elena, a column of crosshatched diamonds and fans emphasized the hobstar (375). Ramona sharply joined shallow miters with rectangles of cross-hatching and gave this combination equal importance with the circled hobstars (376). Pointed ovals united hobstars in Cornell (377). Hobstars formed the border for notched miters in Clifton (378).

Pairpoint more than met the competition with heavily cut glass and unique designs. The minute cutting of hobstars and cane in Myrtle rivaled the work of Hoare (379). The ovals that framed hobstars with single star centers in Berwick closely resembled the designs of Sinclaire (380). Potomska challenged the flashed stars of Meriden (381).

In the late Brilliant Period, Pairpoint returned to simple patterns. The shape rather than the Strawberry-Diamond pattern made the piece outstanding (382). Raised Diamond revived the pointed diamond motif (383). A large pointed diamond motif took the name of Block Diamond (384). Recently we found a cigarette lighter, never used, in the Block Diamond. Innovative shapes give a good clue to the glass of Mt. Washington and Pairpoint.

372. A comport in Saratoga shown in Pairpoint catalog.

373. An ice cream tray in Salem, Pairpoint catalog.

374. An ice cream tray, 14 inches, in Silver Leaf, identified in Pairpoint catalog.

375. A jug with silver top in Elena, Pairpoint catalog.

376. A catsup bottle in Ramona, Pairpoint catalog.

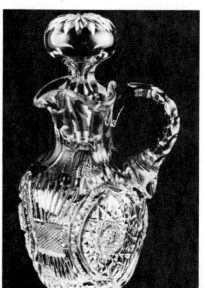

377. A relish or pickle dish in Cornell, Pairpoint catalog.

378. A jug in Clifton shown in Pairpoint catalog.

379. An 11-inch bowl in Myrtle, Pairpoint catalog.

380. A 12-inch low bowl in Berwick by Pairpoint catalog.

382. A cheese plate and cover in Strawberry-Diamond illustrated in Pairpoint catalog.

381. A flower center in Potomska illustrated in Pairpoint catalog.

384. A cigarette holder in Block Diamond with metal holder and illustrated in Pairpoint catalog.

383. A decanter in Raised Diamond, Pairpoint catalog.

PITKIN & BROOKS
Chicago, Illinois, 1872–1920

This company advertised three grades of cut glass: imported made abroad from the company's designs, standard that equaled cut glass sold generally throughout the United States, and P & B grade with a guarantee of high quality. The imported pieces, according to the catalogs, included small items such as salt dips, bud vases, or knife rests. Larger pieces—bonbons, nappies, carafes, jugs, and bowls—came under the standard and P & B quality.

From the catalogs came these identifications of P & B quality glass. Unlike catalogs of other companies, Pitkin & Brooks made interesting comments about featured patterns shown in numerous shapes. About Mars, a pointed loops and hobstar pattern, the statement read, "very bright and very cheap (385). "Line not extensive but . . . very good value" referred to Empress, a pointed loops and sunburst pattern (386).

The company cut most of the basic miter outlines. Carolyn, consisting of the Gothic arch and pinwheels, drew this comment: ". . . not new . . . but a very beautiful pattern." (387). About Sunburst the catalog stated, "A very popular pattern at moderate cost" (388). Two patterns in border and notched miters received no special comment: Prism (389) and Derby (390).

385. A 7-inch plate in Mars as seen in 1907 Pitkin & Brooks catalog.

386. Nappy bowl in Empress, 1907 Pitkin & Brooks catalog.

387. Oval bowl in Carolyn, 1907 Pitkin & Brooks catalog.

388. A jug on foot in Sunburst, 1907 Pitkin & Brooks catalog.

389. Ice tub in Prism, 1907 Pitkin & Brooks catalog.

390. A footed punch bowl in Derby, Pitkin & Brooks catalog.

QUAKER CITY CUT GLASS COMPANY
Philadelphia, Pennsylvania, 1902–1927

This company rivaled Libbey in elaborate cutting and Pairpoint in outstanding shapes. In fact, it recycled some of the old Libbey patterns and gave them new names. Like Libbey it cut both the hobstar and pinwheel extensively. The company did interchange the dominant motifs of hobstars and pinwheels but identified both patterns by the same name. In Primrose (391) and Whirlwind (392) the pinwheel dominated smaller hobstars.

Three patterns depended on the pointed oval to join the major motifs. In Angora (393) and Eden (394), the ovals linked hobstars. Intersecting ovals unified the hobstar clusters of Marlborough (395). Roosevelt illustrated minute cutting of pinwheels, hobstars, and intervening cane pointed ovals (396). A bonbon in Mystic emphasized hobstars in a bar outline and a combination of cane and beading (397).

391. A jug in Primrose, Quaker City catalog.

392. A footed bowl in Whirlwind, Quaker City catalog.

393. A comport in Angora, Quaker City catalog.

394. A flower mug in Eden, Quaker City catalog.

395. A low bowl in Marlborough, Quaker City catalog.

396. A revolving punch bowl containing three parts in Roosevelt, Quaker City catalogs.

397. A bonbon in Mystic, Quaker City catalog.

H. P. SINCLAIRE & COMPANY
Corning, New York, 1904–1929

Sinclaire so highly stylized his patterns that they stood out from those of other companies. You can arrange his glass into six basic groups. The first group emphasized geometric cutting. Prisms developed a row outline into a detailed pattern (398). Saturn flashed stars in the center of a hobstar wreath (399). Assyrian separated rows of rosettes with clear miters (400). Pointed ovals with notched and flashed fans formed the swirl outline of Hiawatha (401).

Sinclaire utilized the hobstar as a border on several patterns in group two. Olympian used the pointed oval to stress the hobstar border and cluster center (402). Bristol alternated a small 8-point star with the hobstar for a border (403). In pattern #98, hobstars bordered notched miters (404). Stars, Pillars, & Engraving used a double hobstar border around the miters (405). Hobstars appeared as a border in No. 11 & Engraving (406).

In group three, repetitive motifs in row outline dominated the pattern. Bengal used three rows and then reversed the sequence (407). Sinclaire also cut Bengal with a floral engraving called Bengal & Engraving (408).

A number of Sinclaire's patterns combined a floral or leafy engraved border with a geometric motif for group four. Denver used such a border with a fan

398. A demijohn signed Sinclaire in Prisms with lock and key, inventory pictures and signed.

399. A 12-inch tray in Saturn by Sinclaire, inventory pictures.

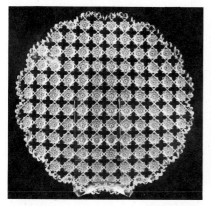

400. A 14-inch tray in Assyrian by Sinclaire, inventory pictures and signed.

401. A 7½-inch plate in Hiawatha, signed Sinclaire, inventory pictures.

402. A 7½-inch plate in Olympian by Sinclaire, inventory pictures.

403. A 10-inch plate in Bristol by Sinclaire, inventory pictures.

404. A 9-inch plate signed Sinclaire in pattern #98, inventory pictures.

405. A 10-inch plate in Stars, Pillars, & Engraving by Sinclaire, inventory pictures.

406. A footed cream in No. 11 & Engraving by Sinclaire, inventory pictures.

407. Footed punch bowl in Bengal by Sinclaire, inventory pictures.

408. A flower center in Bengal & Engraving by Sinclaire, inventory pictures.

409. A 7-inch plate in Denver and signed Sinclaire, inventory pictures.

and hobstar pattern (409). Snow Flakes & Holly combined holly with single stars and hobstars (410). Plaid & Thistle placed the single stars and hobstars in crosshatched squares (411). Engraving enhanced Russian & Border (412). In a pattern called Cut & Engraving No. 1 the floral design formed a border for fans and hobstars (413).

In the fifth group, Sinclaire cut floral designs within various shapes of medallions or frames. Adam emphasized two styles of flowers (414). One version of Diamonds & Silver Threads used medallions (415); another framed the flowers with ovals and hexagons (416).

For group six, Sinclaire combined designs from nature with geometric motifs. Arcadian alternated flowers within Gothic arches and added a hobstar and fan border (417). Pattern No. 1021 used a floral design to join the hobstars (418). Sinclaire frequently created new patterns by changing the engraved parts. Pattern No. 100 alternated a section of fruit with one of rosettes (419). He retained the geometric cut but changed the engraving for No. 99, Lace Hobnails & Cornflowers, and Lace Hobnails and Fruit. Sinclaire's training as a naturalist provides the identification to many of his patterns.

410. A 14-inch tray in Snow Flakes & Holly by Sinclaire, inventory pictures.

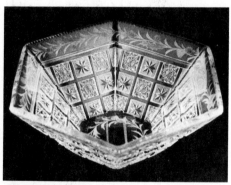

411. An 8-inch bowl in Plaid & Thistle by Sinclaire, inventory pictures.

12. A nappy signed Sinclaire in Russian & Border, inventory pictures.

413. A 7-inch plate signed Sinclaire in Cut & Engraving No. 1, inventory pictures.

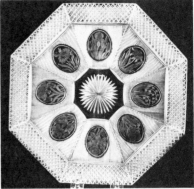

414. A 10-inch plate in Adam by Sinclaire, inventory pictures.

415. An octagonal plate in Diamonds and Silver Threads by Sinclaire, inventory pictures.

416. A 14-inch tray signed Sinclaire in Diamonds & Silver Threads with different flowers from 415, Sinclaire inventory pictures.

417. A plate signed Sinclaire in Arcadian, inventory pictures.

418. A teapot in pattern No. 1021 and signed Sinclaire, inventory pictures.

419. A footed punch bowl in pattern No. 100 and signed Sinclaire, inventory pic-

L. STRAUS & SONS
New York, New York, 1888–?

Material for identifying the pattern names of cut glass by Straus has come from one catalog and magazine advertisements. These designers signed the patent records: Benjamin Franklin Davies, Hermann Siegel, and Herman Richman. They created patterns comparable to the best of any company. The catalog identified two row outlines. Warren consisted of crosscut diamonds and single stars (420), while rows of crosscut and crosshatched diamonds alternate with single stars in Venetian (421). A pointed loops outline joined alternating crosshatched diamonds and elongated hobstars in Imperial (422). La Rabida linked hobstars with pointed ovals of cane (423).

420. A 10-inch bowl in Warren by Straus, 1893 catalog.

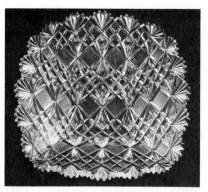

421. A 12-inch square bowl in Venetian by Straus, 1893 catalog.

422. An 11½-inch oval bowl in Imperial, 1893 catalog.

423. A 20-inch lamp signed Straus in La Rabida, 1893 catalog.

TUTHILL CUT GLASS COMPANY,
Corning, New York, 1895–1900
Middletown, New York, 1900–1923

Wallace Turner made the identifications of patterns for us, and most of the pieces come from his extensive collection. He has spent years studying Tuthill glass, interviewing former workers and family members, checking old records of the company. He has opened the Tuthill Cut Glass Company Museum at Stepping Stone Inn in Middletown, New York. You can visit it between the hours of 9:30 A.M. and 4:30 P.M. on weekdays.

When Charles Tuthill first opened a cutting shop in Corning, he created geometric patterns that resembled those of other companies. A simple geometric pattern placed a wide border of crosscut diamonds around a single star and called the design Quilted-Diamond and Star (424). Cluster focused on hobstars (425). A band of flat stars and intersecting miters formed a border for notched miters in Rosette (426). A blazed star dominated Geometric Rose (427).

Possibly Rex (503), Wheel, and Shell (428) rank as Tuthill's best-known patterns. Tuthill cut the shell in three different versions: a shape similar to a heart, panels radiating from a hobstar (429), panels leading to a double star (430).

424. A 9-inch plate in Quilted-Diamond and Star by Tuthill.

425. Celery tray in Cluster by Tuthill.

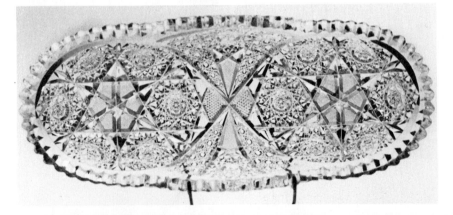

426. Comport in Rosette, signed Tuthill.

427. A vase signed Tuthill in Geometric Rose.

428. A bonbon signed Tuthill in Shell.

429. A slightly different Shell pattern signed Tuthill.

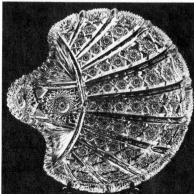

430. A tray in Tuthill's Shell with double hobstars.

113

After Tuthill moved his shop to Middletown, he combined intaglio with geometric cutting. Like Sinclaire, he framed flowers and fruit with geometric borders. Russian formed the border for Pansy and Russian (431). He cut a band of hobstars around Fern (432), Rosaceae and Flowering Raspberry (433), and Intaglio Grape (434). Evidently Intaglio Grape proved very popular as we found it in a number of collections.

Hobstars separated the flowers in several patterns. Tuthill repeated the same hobstar motifs in ovals for Lilliaceae (435) and Poppy (436). Dahlia relied on an 8-point star in the geometric part (437). In Athena (438) and Diamond Point (439) decorated and floral bars framed the hobstars.

431. A tray in Pansy and Russian by Tuthill.

432. A Nabisco tray in Fern cut by Harry Hornbaker for Tuthill.

433. A 10-inch plate in Rosaceae and Flowering Raspberry by Tuthill.

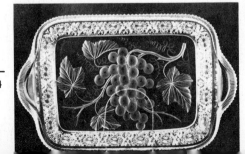

434. A tray in Intaglio Grape with stem up by Tuthill.

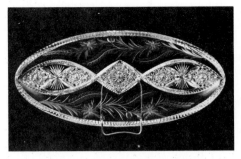

435. Relish dish in Lilliaceae by Tuthill.

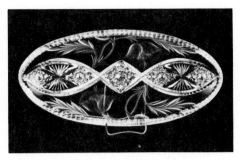

436. Relish tray in Poppy by Tuthill.

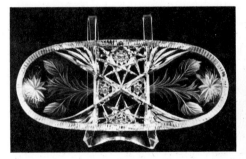

437. Celery in Dahlia by Tuthill.

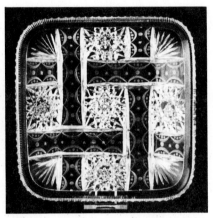

438. A card tray in Athena by Tuthill.

439. A spoon tray in Diamond Point by Tuthill.

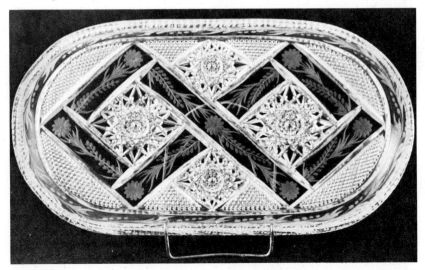

A number of different shapes and patterns took the name of Primrose. In one pattern, Tuthill alternated the Primrose with a panel of crosshatching and flat stars (440). Primroses filled the spaces between bars with hobstars in Primrose and Bar (441). In two other geometric patterns Primrose formed the border (442 and 443). Tuthill introduced two slightly different motifs in Swirl Primrose (444 and 445).

The company also glorified the wild rose in several patterns. In the wild rose motif, the five petals turned over at the edge. (The primrose contained six petals.) Three different patterns used the wild rose: crosshatching framed the flower (446), another used crosshatched triangles between the flowers (447), and a third combined the wild rose with hobstars (448).

Tuthill combined fruits with hobstars. The pattern took the name of the fruit depicted. In Apple, the fruit formed the center (449), but in Plum it served as the border for hobstars (450).

Unless the item contained a signature, you most likely will not recognize Tuthill's geometric patterns. His combination of geometric with flowers or fruit you can easily identify.

440. A jug in which Primrose alternates with geometric motif, by Tuthill.

441. A presentation tray or gift with W for Wiggins in Primrose and Bar by Tuthill.

443. A footed rose globe with a Primrose border by Tuthill.

442. A jug with a Primrose border by Tuthill.

444 and 445. A 10-inch plate in Swirl Primrose and a 9-inch low bowl in Swirl Primrose but with a slightly different motif on the swirl, both by Tuthill.

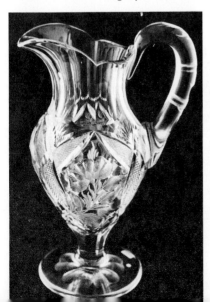

446. A footed jug that combines the Wild Rose with geometric motifs, signed Tuthill.

117

447. A 10-inch plate in Wild Rose by Tuthill.

448. A covered dish in Wild Rose and signed Tuthill.

449. A footed bowl signed Tuthill in Apple.

450. A vase in Plum by Tuthill, but with a missing part.

UNGER BROTHERS
Newark, New Jersey, 1901–1918

Unger Brothers started as a company that produced household wares in silver. The two Unger catalogs divided the illustrations into sections for silver and for glass. We have found very few pieces of Unger in collections. The patterns identified emphasized hobstars as the dominant motifs. La Voy used hobstars with a combination Gothic arch and star outline (451). Fontenoy joined hobstars with bands of nailheads in a star outline (452). Crosshatched triangles and notched miters emphasized the hobstars in Undine (453). A panel of crosshatched diamonds alternated with one of notched miters in Hobart (454). Duchess, a very detailed pattern, cut every space on the blank (455).

451. A 12-inch plate in La Voy by Unger, in catalog.

452. An 8-inch bowl in Fontenoy, pictured in Unger catalog.

453. A jug in Undine identified by Unger catalog.

454. A jug in Hobart shown in Unger catalog.

455. A 14-inch tray in Duchess, 1906 Unger catalog.

LESSER-KNOWN COMPANIES

With the exceptions of Parsche and Maple City Glass Company we found very little information on the following companies. Various collections contained only a very few pieces. Perhaps more material will become available in the future.

C. G. ALFORD & COMPANY
New York, New York, 1872–1918

The one available catalog by Alford, a manufacturer's agent and retail outlet, illustrated mainly standard patterns. Criterion placed pinwheels between pointed ovals (456). Four ovals met at a point and created spaces for hobstars in Burgundy (457). A border of elongated hobstars and notched miters formed Brunswick (458).

456. A whiskey jug in Criterion in 1904 Alford catalog.

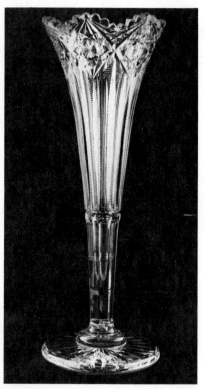

458. A vase in Brunswick, 1904 Alford catalog.

457. A decanter in Burgundy, 1904 Alford catalog.

M. J. AVERBECK MANUFACTURER
New York, New York, 1892–1923

Averbeck, primarily a wholesale jewelry store, advertised in catalog 104 that it produced its own glass at a factory in Honesdale, Pennsylvania. Most of the patterns showed quality cut in high brilliance. Acme consisted of pointed loops with hobstars (459). Cape Town contained bars of hobstars and feathering (460). Crosshatching and cane linked hobstars and 8-point stars in London (461). The catalog illustrated two slightly different patterns in London and four in Ruby.

459. A 14-inch ice cream tray in Acme, #104 Averbeck catalog.

460. A 14½-inch ice cream tray in Cape Town, #104 Averbeck catalog.

461. Footed celery in London, #104 Averbeck catalog.

A. L. BLACKMER COMPANY
New Bedford, Massachusetts, 1894–1916

Blackmer produced standard, well-balanced designs in the brilliant tradition. The 1906-1907 catalog featured Columbia (73). Hobstars dominated Concord (462) and Redmond (463). Diamonds of crosshatching formed Ruby (464).

463. A comport in Redmond pictured in 1906–1907 Blackmer catalog.

464. A cream with a set in Ruby by Blackmer, 1906–1907 catalog.

462. A decanter in Concord shown in 1906–1907 Blackmer catalog.

ELMIRA CUT GLASS COMPANY
Elmira, New York, 1893–1916

Unfortunately this company numbered all patterns. We found six different shapes in various collections for #33. Some pieces with this number added fans (465) while others used only the reverse fan (466). Hobstars made up most of the pattern for #80 (467).

465. A mug in #33 with added fans at top, pictured in Elmira catalog.

466. A comport in #33 without the fans but illustrated in the Elmira catalog.

467. A bonbon in #80 and shown in Elmira catalog.

IRVING CUT GLASS COMPANY, INC.
Honesdale, Pennsylvania, 1900–1930

This company did much cutting of flowers on figured blanks. William H. Hawken, who apprenticed with Clark, designed and cut the two patterns shown here. Doris combined flowers with a variance of cane (468) and Combination Rose used a button border and a stylized rose (469).

468. A celery in Doris as seen in Irving catalog.

469. An ice tub in Combination Rose, pictured in Irving catalog.

LAUREL CUT GLASS COMPANY
Jermyn, Pennsylvania, 1903–1920

Laurel produced brilliant cut glass at first and then turned to flowers and figured blanks. Eunice focused the pattern around a cluster of flat stars and crosshatched diamonds (470). Pointed ovals of nailheads, crosshatching, and hobstars combined with large hobstars to form Audrey (471). The bars in Everett alternated a feather with a crosshatched pointed oval (472).

470. A sugar to a set in Eunice by Laurel, 1907 catalog.

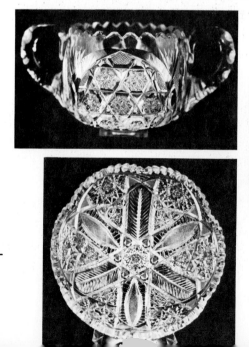

471. A spoon dish in Audrey, 1907 Laurel catalog.

472. An 8-inch bowl in Everett, 1907 Laurel catalog.

LIBERTY CUT GLASS COMPANY
Egg Harbor City, New Jersey, 1902–1931

Although the catalog illustrated numerous patterns, we have seen only one, Princeton, a star outline accented with hobstar (474).

LINFORD CUT GLASS COMPANY
Jamestown, New York, 1895–1902

A Gothic arch and hobstars characterized Nottingham (473).

LUZERNE CUT GLASS COMPANY
Pittston, Pennsylvania, ?–1930

We found only two pieces of cut glass by this company in spite of the large number of patterns shown in the catalog. Oddly enough, one collector owned both of them. Electra has pointed bars of hobstars and pinwheels as the major motif (475). Buzzstars alternated with smaller hobstars in the Gothic arch outline of Myron (476).

473. A bonbon in Nottingham, Linford catalog.

474. A nappy in Princeton in Liberty catalog.

475. A 14½-inch tray in Electra, shown in Luzerne catalog.

476. A 14-inch tray in Myron, found in Luzerne catalog.

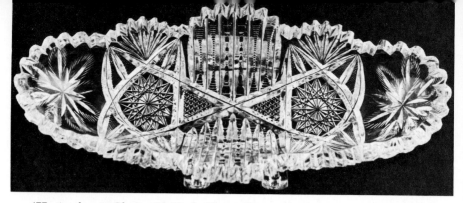

477. A celery in Gloria, #3 Maple City catalog.

MAPLE CITY GLASS COMPANY
Hawley, Pennsylvania, 1900–?

We found several signed pieces in a number of collections but a catalog name for only one, Gloria, in the three available catalogs. This pattern featured a blazed star and flat stars as the dominant motifs (477).

C. F. MONROE COMPANY
Meriden, Connecticut, 1880–1916

Along with standard cut glass items, the catalog illustrated some interesting novelties, such as the Y. W. Bell (478).

F. X. PARSCHE & SONS COMPANY
Chicago, Illinois, 1876–

This company still operates at the same address under the supervision of Donald Parsche and his brother, Russ (479). A chain of hobstars and curved miters formed the Laurel Wreath pattern by this company (480). Donald Parsche has shared with us his grandfather's production notes on time required to produce certain patterns and shapes by the dozen:

PATTERNS AND SHAPES	ROUGHING HOURS	SMOOTHING HOURS
8-inch bowl Empire	30	50–60
Cyrano sugar and cream	48	48–72
Sunburst carafe	15	15–20
Sunburst celery	3	18
Sunburst decanter	28	28–40

A two-piece punch bowl, 12 inches in diameter, in Sunburst, required twelve hours for roughing and twelve to fourteen for smoothing. Parsche went on to explain, "You will find most of the help worked for about sixteen dollars a week." An 8-ounce cologne cut in Heart, for instance, cost as follows: blank 80¢, roughing 25¢, and smoothing 65¢. In addition to all these costs, the design needed drawing and acid polishing.

478. A bell by Monroe, identified as Y. W., #6 catalog.

479. The cutting shop of Parsche & Sons Company today in Chicago. Pictured are two sons, Donald and Russell.

480. A jug in Laurel Wreath and pictured in Parsche catalog.

PHOENIX GLASS COMPANY
Monaca, Pennsylvania, 1880–1930

The 1893 catalog of this company illustrated a selection of gas and electric lighting fixtures in a ball and bowl shape. A ball in Phoenix consisted of hobstars and crosshatched bars (481). A bowl in the Russian pattern the company called Star and Hobnail (482).

481. A light ball in Phoenix, shown in 1893 Phoenix catalog.

482. A light bowl in Star and Hobnail, 1893 Phoenix catalog.

STERLING CUT GLASS COMPANY
Cincinnati, Ohio, 1902–1950

A 1913 catalog pictured two patterns we found in two collections. Eden combined fruit and bands of crosscut diamonds (483). In Regal a border of wild rose framed the center square of hobstars (484).

483. A 10-inch plate in Eden by Sterling, illustration in catalog.

484. A 10-inch plate in Regal by Sterling, seen in catalog.

TAYLOR BROTHERS
Philadelphia, Pennsylvania, 1902–1915

In researching this company, we met Florence Taylor Vay, the daughter of one of the brothers. She showed us her christening cup cut by her father in the Bellevue pattern with a colonial rim (485). She also has preserved a Taylor Brothers catalog from which we identified several pieces. In Arcadia, a blazed buzz dominated circles of hobstars (486). Blazed stars alternated with panels of crosshatching and hobstars in Palm (487).

485. A sugar and cream in Bellevue, Taylor Brothers catalog.

486. A 10½-inch tray in Arcadia by Taylor Brothers, shown in catalog.

487. A 12-inch tray in Palm by Taylor Brothers, illustrated in catalog.

CANADIAN COMPANIES

A good deal of Canadian glass passes as American. If the company bought blanks from American firms, you will have difficulty recognizing the glass as Canadian. Blanks from Val St. Lambert and Baccarat have a slight grayish tint. Your other positive proof consists of a signature.

GUNDY-CLAPPERTON COMPANY
Toronto, Canada, 1905–1931

C. H. Clapperton served an apprenticeship of ten years at the Libbey Glass Company before he opened his own cutting shop. The elaborate patterns of his company showed the Libbey influence. Touchstone favored the hobstar dominance (488). Triple fans and nailhead diamonds united hobstars in Norman (489). Elongated fans sprout from a row of flat stars in Classic (490).

488. A celery in Touchstone by Gundy-Clapperton, 1909 catalog and with signature.

489. A fern holder in Norman by Gundy-Clapperton, 1909 catalog and signed.

490. A decanter in Classic, signed and in 1909 Gundy-Clapperton catalog.

RODEN BROTHERS
Toronto, Canada, 1894–?

We identified three pieces signed by this company from a 1917 catalog. Fans and single stars served as a minor motif combination for the hobstars in pattern #251 (491). Queenston contained rows of fans, crosshatched diamonds, and single stars that encircled a star outline (492). Oakly designated a very unusual engraved and geometric-cut pattern (493).

A few of these patterns you may already know by the catalog name. We included them for the collector or dealer who does not know them and to give a complete analysis of style characteristic of various companies. Most of these patterns have never been identified by catalog name. May you match pieces of your cut glass to these catalog names.

491. A lamp in pattern #251, Roden Brothers, 1917 catalog.

492. An 8-inch bowl in Queenston by Roden, 1917 catalog.

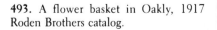

493. A flower basket in Oakly, 1917 Roden Brothers catalog.

4

Pattern Puzzles

A dealer at a show displayed a bowl and an ice cream tray with identical patterns and asked us why the signatures differed.

A collector brought two almost identical bowls to a lecture we gave on cut glass and wanted to know if the same company cut both.

An appraiser telephoned and asked, "Which of these two names do I use for this pattern? I have learned one only to find it has another."

In identifying cut glass as to source and pattern, you run into a number of intriguing puzzles such as these. Research revealed that the factories and cutting shops themselves caused many of these pattern puzzles.

COMPANY PRACTICES

As the demand for American cut glass increased in both the domestic and foreign market, companies needed more patterns. To create new patterns they slightly altered their own and those of other companies. In some cases they cut the same pattern but changed the name. Other times they retained the name but cut a different pattern.

ALTERED PATTERNS

The designer of a pattern made a sketch first and then fit it to the shape. A few pattern makers preferred to create the design directly on the glass. To fit the pattern to a different shape the designer drew the pattern on a heavy drawing paper called a template and wrapped this around the object, cutting it to fit the shape. Such adaptations naturally changed the pattern. You can easily recognize the Chrysanthemum pattern on a plate (494), but few could identify this jug without the aid of an illustration in a Hawkes catalog (495).

In addition to the change by shape, a buyer placing a large order might request certain alterations in a basic pattern—for instance a hobstar instead of a pinwheel. Management then directed the designer to make this change in pattern. If the company received repeat orders for this altered pattern, then they pictured it in the catalog. As Bill Iorio pointed out, "The name of the game was to sell."

This situation might explain why an Egginton catalog showed several slight changes in the Creswick pattern. In one illustration of a flower center the crosshatched diamonds of the star outline separated the hobstars at the top of the design (496), while on a pickle dish the crosshatched diamonds appeared at the base of the piece (842). Two different sugar and cream sets in the catalog illustrated this change.

In another example, an 1896 Clark catalog pictured the star border on the Palmetto pattern differently on a bowl and on a jug. The jug used elongated hobstars in a diamond frame for the border (497). The border on the bowl

494. A 7-inch plate signed Hawkes in Chrysanthemum.

495. A jug in Chrysanthemum that shows changes in pattern for shape.

496. A flower center in Creswick and signed Egginton shows the crosshatched diamond at the top of the design.

497. A jug in Palmetto by Clark in 1896 catalog uses a border of elongated hobstars.

placed a split diamond between the elongated hobstars (498). The shape of the two pieces would not necessitate any changes in this pattern. A Quaker City catalog showed the Carlysle pattern cut either with a pinwheel or a hobstar as the dominant motif.

If two factories each cut one part of a two-piece set, slight changes might result. On a butter tub and plate the miters differed. The parallel miters on the tub have notches while those on the plate have none (74).

A producer of cut glass might simplify a pattern to cut costs. In 1903 Libbey introduced a pattern called New Brilliant, composed of notched miters and a combination of fan, crosshatched diamonds, and flat star (499). Two years later the company simplified the pattern (500).

Usually when a designer created an original pattern, he secured a patent and assigned it to the company for which he worked. These patents extended for periods of three, five, and seven years. At the end of the designated period, the pattern became public domain, allowing other companies to cut it.

Shops too small to hire a professional designer did not wait for the expiration date of the patent on a popular pattern. They broke the patent with minor changes in the pattern. Hawkes's Festoon as shown in its catalog has two overlapping squares that formed an 8-point star. Two sizes of hobstars circled this center star (501). A similar piece, often mistaken for Festoon, has two overlapping triangles that form a 6-point star with a border of only one size of hobstars (502).

498. The border on a bowl also shown in 1896 catalog uses a split diamond between the elongated hobstars.

499. The jug signed Libbey in New Brilliant, 1905 catalog, shows heavier cutting.

500. A jug in the simplified pattern of New Brilliant shown in 1908 Libbey catalog.

501. An 8-inch square dish in Festoon by Hawkes.

502. A 7½-inch plate in a pattern similar to Festoon.

Itinerant cutters made breaking a patent very simple as they traveled from job to job. Patterns they had previously cut they could change easily and frequently did. Actually, they found a job sooner if they had worked under top pattern makers such as William C. Anderson, Thomas Singleton, Benjamin Davies, James J. O'Conner, William Marrett—to name a few. These cutters knew the top patterns of the designer so well they could make slight alterations that went unnoticed by the buyer.

These slight changes you can observe in a number of popular patterns. Possibly such a cutter changed the position of the fans in Rex by Tuthill. Rex showed fans cut within a crosshatched triangle (503). The non-Rex placed the fans on either side of the crosshatched triangle (504).

503. A 9½-inch bowl in Rex by Tuthill.

504. A vase that places the fans at the side of the crosshatched diamond, in a non-Rex pattern.

The popularity of Libbey patterns led to frequent copying by other companies. A number of companies altered the very popular Corinthian pattern by Libbey (505) with a change in the crosscut diamond motif. Straus substituted cane and Hoare the nailhead diamond for the crosscut diamond (506). The original Kimberly pattern by Libbey contained a straight miter outline of intersecting triangles that formed a star. Double fans accented the points (507). An adapted pattern used intersecting squares with curved sides and no fans (508).

A company often created other patterns from their own popular ones. Most of you will easily recognize Queens by Hawkes. In this pattern panels of punties alternated with those of hobstars (509). The company then cut a similar pattern named Kings with rows of hobstars, punties, fans, and 8-point stars (510). Hawkes also created the Princess pattern by changing the hobstars of Queens to 5-point stars.

The adaptations did not end there. In Brunswick, Hawkes placed vertical lines across two miters, then notched two (511). Marquis differed in that it alternated three notched miters with a clear one (512). Usually Brunswick and Marquis have only one band of hobstars near the top of the piece, but on large items Hawkes cut both an upper and lower border.

505. A 10-inch plate in Corinthian, signed Libbey, 1896 catalog.

506. A comport signed Hoare in a Corinthian type pattern.

507. An 8-inch bowl in Kimberly, 1893 catalog.

508. A low bowl in an adaptation of the Kimberly pattern.

509. A 7½-inch plate signed Hawkes in Queens.

510. A 15½-inch plate in Kings, signed by Hawkes.

511. A jug signed Hawkes in Brunswick.

512. A jug signed Hawkes in Marquis.

To add more confusion to the identification of patterns, a company might advertise a pattern under a particular name, and then a few years later cut a completely different pattern under the same name. Before 1900, a Hawkes catalog illustrated the Imperial pattern with large hobstars (513). Several years later the company designed a different pattern with triple miters and small hobstars and named it Imperial (514).

Hawkes did this again with another pattern. On May 8, 1888, Hawkes patented a pattern called Devonshire, in which double fans joined a diamond

513. An early Imperial pattern by Hawkes, identified by catalog.

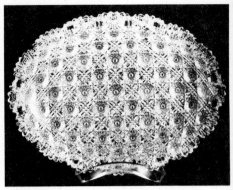

514. A later Imperial pattern signed Hawkes and identified by catalog.

515. A 10-inch low bowl, signed Hawkes and in later Devonshire pattern, located in catalog.

516. A jug signed Clark in Huyler but advertised as Rose, 1903 catalog.

518. A jug in Harvard, 1893 Libbey catalog.

517. A catsup bottle in Anson, in Hawkes catalog.

combination consisting of four parts. After 1900, Hawkes used the name Devonshire on an entirely different pattern. In this pattern large crosscut diamonds replaced the more ornate combination (515).

Other times a company might designate a pattern by one name and several years later change it but not the pattern. In 1901, a Clark catalog introduced a pattern as Huyler, but a 1909 advertisement in *Ladies' Home Journal* called the design Rose (516).

Hawkes also changed the name on patterns but not the design. He usually described and named the pattern in the letters patent that accompanied the application. In his letters patent dated April 14, 1896, he stated:

> The leading features of my design consist of a large double cross or asterisk figure covering the body of the dish, having radial pointed arms, a central rosette at the crossing of the arms forming the body of the figure, crosshatching on the arms and double lines extending lengthwise of the arms, thus representing leaves having stems, checkered cutting at the inner ends of the arms and foils between the arms having rosettes, thus forming what I call "Aberdeen" design.

A later Hawkes catalog, however, pictured this same pattern as Anson (517).

Several established companies cut highly similar patterns. Harvard by Libbey alternated the crosscut diamond with the crosshatched one (518). A similar pattern by Dorflinger used crosshatched diamonds only (519). You can easily confuse the two patterns unless you see them together.

Hawkes's Gladys resembled an early one by Tuthill in that both designs used the 8-point star and crosshatched diamonds. The Tuthill pattern has no fans on the border and space around the hobstar in the center (520). The Hawkes design enlarged the center hobstar so as to leave no uncut surface and added a fan border (521). Since Charles Tuthill operated a cutting shop in Corning between 1895 and 1900, cutting glass in the same locale might suggest a possible reason for the similarity.

Most major companies offered to cut replacements of broken pieces. If a company had cut the pattern originally, the replacement oridinarily matched the design. Frequently the owner sent only a small, broken part of the item for matching. If the company did not cut or know the pattern, the craftsman duplicated it as best he could; but often the design did not match exactly. On a set of tumblers in Clark's Clarion pattern the pinwheel swirls clockwise on five and counterclockwise on the sixth (522).

Occasionally, you run into a piece that could have resulted from one or more of these situations. Two different owners, one of a nappy and the other of a plate, identified the pieces as Nautilus by Hawkes. A Hawkes catalog identified the pattern on the nappy as the true Nautilus (523). The plate differed in the Gothic arches, the fans, and the borders of the circles (524). Another Nautilus-type plate we saw left the outside rim of the interlocking circles undecorated. Recently we heard of a young cutter in New Hampshire who cut a Nautilus pattern. We saw one of his pieces that looked fairly good until we compared it to the authentic Nautilus.

519. A vase in a pattern similar to Harvard but cut by Dorflinger.

520. A 7-inch plate in an early pattern by Tuthill.

521. A 7½-inch plate signed Hawkes in the Gladys pattern.

522. Two tumblers with pinwheels turning in opposite directions, Clarion pattern by Clark, 1905 catalog.

523. A nappy signed Hawkes in Nautilus pattern, identified by catalog.

524. An 11½-inch tray in a pattern similar to Nautilus.

No doubt you can find other altered patterns. These do challenge you to accurately identify the design. Certainly they make you more observant of details and warn not to jump to quick identifications.

DUPLICATE PATTERNS

Perhaps the duplication of patterns, whether or not companies changed the name, caused as many puzzles as did alterations.

Five different companies produced a pattern where triple miters framed hobstars. Hawkes, as mentioned, took the name from a previous pattern, Imperial (514). Egginton named it Calvé. According to Miss Lucille Egginton, her father greatly admired the Metropolitan Opera diva Emma Calvé, for whom he named the pattern. Hoare called the pattern Kohinoor for the largest diamond in the British crown (525). You will find slight differences in various cuttings of this pattern by Hoare, mainly in the way the miters frame the hobstars (526). Parsche listed the pattern as Star Hob-Nail while Dorflinger numbered it #210. You may have heard the descriptive name "trellis variation."

Collectors and dealers can easily mistake some slightly similar patterns for this triple miters and hobstar design. Mt. Washington used the same triple miters but substituted an 8-point star for the hobstar of the other pattern. The company called this pattern by three different names even in the same catalog: B & T, Three Cut Octagon, and #60 (527). A later Pairpoint catalog gave the name of Three Cut Octagon to a pattern that substituted a crosshatched button for the hobstar. Since Hawkes also cut this pattern with the crosshatched button as #3709, either company could have produced the jug shown here (528).

Trellis used a clear miter to form squares for the hobstars. Hoare and Egginton identified the clear miter pattern as Trellis in their catalog, but Hawkes called the same design Willow in his catalog (529). A Mt. Washington catalog pictured the same pattern as Williams.

Five different companies considered one pattern worth duplicating. In this pattern flashed fans framed two sizes of hobstars (530). Elmira numbered the pattern #28 and Bergen listed it as Vivian in its catalogs. A magazine advertisement for Fry and an Empire catalog identified the pattern as Elsie. Perhaps the close association of Fry with Empire explained part of this duplication. Hoare signed the tray.

Four different companies produced the Renaissance pattern where double horizontal miters form a band around vertical miters (531). Dorflinger, Pitkin & Brooks, and Clark used Renaissance as the name. A Mt. Washington catalog numbered the pattern #33.

Five patterns by Pairpoint appeared in other company catalogs. A pattern with blazed ovals and hobstars Pairpoint listed as Nevada, but Blackmer named it Oxford (532). Pairpoint illustrated a pattern where spaces intervened between a series of five notched miters as Fanchon, but Bergen called it Split and Hollow (533). An 8-point star alternated with a diamond combination in Pairpoint's Doris and Empire's Special (534). Pairpoint named a hobstar and

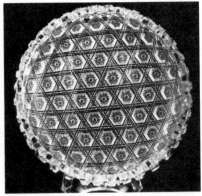

525. An 8-inch bowl signed Hoare in Kohinoor, 1911 catalog.

526. An 8-inch bowl in Kohinoor and signed Hoare, pictured in 1911 catalog.

527. A jug in Three Cut Octagon pattern by Mt. Washington, identified by catalog.

528. A jug in either Three Cut Octagon by Pairpoint or #3708 by Hawkes, identified by catalogs.

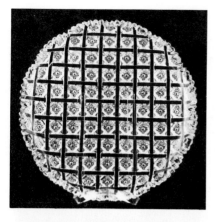

529. A 12-inch tray in Trellis and signed by Egginton. Also called Willow by Hawkes and Williams by Mt. Washington, Trellis by Hoare.

530. A 14-inch tray signed by Hoare, called #28 by Elmira, Vivian by Bergen, and Elsie by Empire and Fry.

531. A tantalus set by Dorflinger in Renaissance pattern, but also cut by Pitkin & Brooks, Clark by same name, numbered #33 by Mt. Washington; catalog identifications.

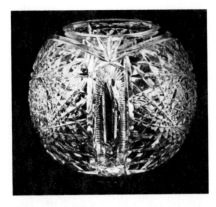

532. A rose globe named Nevada by Pairpoint and Oxford by Blackmer; catalog identification.

533. A nappy in Split and Hollow by Bergen or Fanchon by Pairpoint.

534. A champagne in Doris by Pairpoint or Special by Empire.

535. A jug in Korea by Pairpoint or Baltic by Bergen.

536. A decanter in Oval and Split by Dorflinger or #12 by Pairpoint.

537. A nappy in Troy by Blackmer or Prince by Empire.

crosscut diamond pattern Korea, while Bergen listed it as Baltic (535). Dorflinger referred to a pattern where a horizontal miter separated two rows of punties as Oval and Split, but Pairpoint numbered it #12 (536).

Three patterns illustrated by Blackmer appeared in catalogs of other companies. Blackmer called the pattern Troy while Empire named it Prince (537). The pattern consisted of a star outline with hobstars and fans. Alford listed as Trieste a pattern that placed a notched miter border around a bar outline, but Blackmer chose the name of Regal for the same design (538). Blackmer listed a pattern with a star and bar outline and hobstars as Emerson; Pitkin & Brooks called the same design Star (539).

In a catalog Pitkin & Brooks complained about other companies copying patterns. One star outline and hobstar pattern which Pitkin & Brooks called Plaza, Elmira numbered as #80, and Monroe listed it as Rockmere (540). A pattern that placed a notched miter border around alternating hobstars and shooting stars, Pitkin & Brooks illustrated as Roland (541). Empire cut the same pattern under the name Plymouth.

When other companies produced duplicate patterns, they made no comment. Empire cut a pattern where notched miters and fans joined large hobstars and called it Japan (542). Hoare listed the same pattern as Japany. Clark referred to a pattern with a major hobstar motif as San Gabriel, but Hoare signed an identical pattern and illustrated it in a catalog as #9921

(543). A pattern with a band of crosscut diamonds and intersecting miters Hawkes listed in a catalog as Cobweb, but Dorflinger numbered it #643 (544).

According to some authorities, Sinclaire and other companies occasionally agreed to let another firm duplicate one of their original patterns. This gave the pattern wider distribution and helped both companies financially. We could find no records to verify this, possibly because they made a verbal agreement. The fact could explain why two companies cut the same pattern.

A number of companies helped each other with orders in case of strikes or to keep their employees working during slack periods. Helping meant loan of craftsmen, use of factory space, or actually doing an entire cutting. When employees struck at Pitkin & Brooks, according to Donald Parsche, his father helped the company catch up on back orders for the Heart pattern (545). "When the men from Pitkin & Brooks came to pick up the glass, they measured each cut to the centimeter and refused to take any that varied from the exact specification," he said.

Parsche sold the rejected pieces of the Heart pattern, but later, on May 14, 1907, he patented his own similar design. The Parsche pattern changed the center of the heart from the hobnail of Pitkin & Brooks to a type of Russian. A Buffalo Cut Glass Company catalog duplicated the Pitkin & Brooks Heart but called the pattern Thistle. A Fry catalog also pictured the same Pitkin & Brooks pattern, but numbered it #175. One collector showed us another heart-type pattern where clear buttons surrounded a single star (546).

Since Hawkes and Hoare often helped each other, this probably explained the signatures on two whiskey tumblers that matched a whiskey jug in Hoare's Monarch pattern. One tumbler contained a Hoare signature and the other that of Hawkes (547).

Often when a pattern maker left a company, he made an agreement to take his designs with him, and the former employer would no longer cut them. For several years both Egginton and Sinclaire worked for Hawkes, so they

538. Nappy signed Alford in Trieste, 1904 catalog; same pattern as Regal by Blackmer, 1906–1907 catalog.

539. A 10-inch tray in Emerson by Blackmer or Star by Pitkin & Brooks.

540. A nappy in Plaza by Pitkin & Brooks, #80 by Elmira, or Rockmere by Monroe.

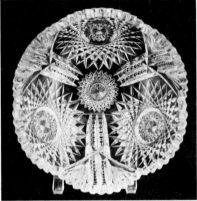

541. A plate in Roland by Pitkin & Brooks or Plymouth by Empire.

542. An 8-inch low bowl in Japany by Hoare or Japan by Empire.

543. A footed punch bowl in San Gabriel by Clark or #9921 by Hoare.

544. A rose globe in Cobweb by Hawkes or #643 by Dorflinger.

probably made this agreement. You'll find some duplication between Hawkes and these two former employees.

Sinclaire cut the same pattern as Hawkes's Marquis but named it Westminister (512). Hawkes called a pattern Hudson in which double fans framed 8-point stars (548). An Egginton catalog listed this pattern as Vendix. Possibly the agreement permitted Hawkes to deplete his stock after Egginton left to form his own company.

Several cutters who cut glass during the Brilliant Period told us that companies cut patterns from public domain and sold them under new names. Quaker City gave the name of Riverton to Libbey's Empress, a pattern of flat stars joined by crosscut diamonds (549). Liberty Cut Glass Company duplicated Clark's Huyler but called it Lester (516).

Egginton's patterns appeared most popular with other companies. His Cluster pattern Elmira numbered #67 (550). This pattern combined the bar outline with the dual motif of hobstars and cane diamonds. We have seen a Straus signature on Egginton's Lotus where hobstars dominate the star outline with three fans (551). Egginton illustrated a hobstar pattern with a star outline as Orleans, but Empire named the design Saxonia (552).

The fact that Pairpoint and Tuthill employed Thomas Mortensen, an engraver, during different years possibly explained why both claimed the same

545. A 9-inch bowl in Heart by Pitkin & Brooks, Thistle by Buffalo, or #175 by Fry.

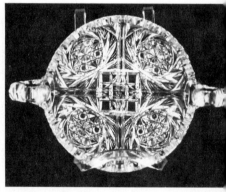

546. A double-handled nappy bowl, 9 inches in diameter, in an unidentified heart-type pattern.

547. A whiskey tumbler in Monarch by Hoare and matching one signed Hawkes.

548. A wine decanter that opens when tilted signed Hawkes in Hudson pattern; same pattern cut by Egginton called Vendix.

549. A flower center in Empress by Libbey, 1898 catalog, called Riverton by Quaker City.

550. A 10-inch tray in Cluster by Egginton but numbered #67 by Elmira.

551. A celery in Lotus by Egginton, but Straus signed this same pattern.

553. A handled nappy in Engraved #41 by Pairpoint or Blackberry by Tuthill.

552. A whipped cream bowl in Orleans by Egginton or Saxonia by Empire.

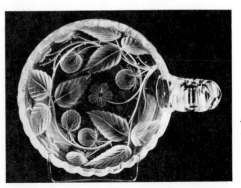

blackberry pattern (553). Pairpoint named it Engraved #41, but Tuthill designated it Blackberry.

Dorothy Daniel gave the name of Harvard to a repetitive pattern of single stars and crosshatched buttons. She attributed the identification to a Hawkes sketchbook. We found this pattern in various catalogs under different names: in Empire as Royal, in Pairpoint as Two Cut Octagon, and in Buffalo as Temple (554).

Several unidentified patterns made slight changes in this basic design which some call chair bottom. One pattern substituted a nailhead button for the single star (555). Another pattern used only the crosshatched button in a border for an engraved design (556). A third added a band of elongated hobstars to the basic pattern (557).

Companies used the same names for a few patterns. Hoare, Libbey, Hawkes, and Pairpoint cut the Basket pattern (558). A number of companies marketed a Flute or Colonial pattern. Hawkes called it Colonial, Libbey referred to it as Plain Flute, Clark named it Flute, Dorflinger used Colonial. The Dorflinger pattern became known as the Prince of Wales because the company cut it for him.

The mended decanter in an unidentified flute pattern pictured here came from the estate of Juliette Gordon Low, organizer of the Girl Scouts. An early mode of mending consisted of drilling holes and inserting staples. This difficult mending method indicates the high value set on cut glass (559).

In these duplications a signature provides the only way to identify the source, but some companies, such as Dorflinger, used paper labels, long ago removed.

554. A decanter in Royal by Empire, Two Cut Octagon by Pairpoint, or Temple by Buffalo.

555. A lamp in a pattern that uses a crosshatched button and nailhead button in a row pattern.

557. A jug with crosshatched buttons and single stars with a border of elongated flat stars and fans.

556. A lamp with crosshatched buttons in a row pattern used as a border.

559. A mended decanter in a flute pattern owned by Juliette Gordon Low, organizer of the Girl Scouts.

558. A demijohn in Basket with lock and key, cut by Hoare, Libbey, Hawkes, or Pairpoint.

MISTAKES BY INDIVIDUALS

While companies did contribute considerably to the difficulties in identification, so do collectors, dealers, and knowledgeable people who write about cut glass.

BLANKS

A number of factories—Libbey, Corning Glass Works, Dorflinger, Union Glass Company, Fry, Pairpoint, to name a few—made blanks and sold them to cutting shops. When a factory produced a distinctive blank, some identify the company that produced the blank rather than the shop that cut the pattern. Some frequently identify the blank for the Eulalia sugar and cream by Libbey by the shape rather than the pattern (560). Others attribute unsigned Egginton to Dorflinger, who made a slightly thinner blank than other companies.

Some factories and cutting shops kept a distinctive blank apparently for their exclusive use. Possibly only Straus, as identified by advertisements and signatures, used the unique blank shown here for a jug (658). According to catalogs and signatures, Libbey alone probably used this distinctive blank for a jug (518). Wallace Turner stated that Tuthill designed his own blanks, as illustrated by this oil (561). If no other used these blanks, then you could possibly conclude that Tuthill also cut the design on the oil in the same shape (562). Shapes do create problems in identification.

560. A sugar and cream in Eulalia by Libbey, an unusual shape.

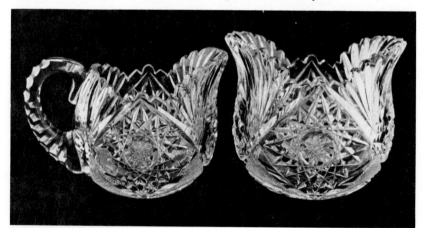

561. An oil in Olive by Tuthill and signed.

562. An unidentified oil in the same shaped blank.

CANADIAN GLASS

A number of Canadian companies—Gundy-Clapperton, Gowans, Kent & Company, Ltd., Roden Brothers, House of Birks, to list a few—bought blanks from firms in the United States and cut their own patterns. We have seen Hawkes's Panel signed with a Canadian signature. Possibly the Canadian company made special arrangements with the American firm to sign the glass or duplicate the pattern.

A Gundy-Clapperton catalog showed a pattern very similar to Hawkes's Panel but called it Coronation. Meriden actually opened a factory in Canada, but you also find its Alhambra pattern signed by Canadian companies. Roden Brothers named the Alhambra pattern Norman (563).

Gowans, Kent cut and signed a pattern described as "expanding star." The signature of this company consisted of a maple leaf with the word "Elite." Some people mistake Elite for the name of the company. The pattern with the Elite signature alternated a nailhead diamond with an elongated hobstar in the points. Double diamonds of crosshatching support the hobstar point and double hobstars the nailhead point. (564).

One pattern signed by Roden and numbered #307-9 cut a reverse fan in the point (565). An unidentified pattern omitted the double hobstars and left the point clear (566). Another pattern, also unidentified, omitted the double hobstars and filled the point with an elongated star (567).

A woman at a cut glass convention told us she saw some loose pages of a Dorflinger catalog at a museum in White Mills, Pennsylvania. One page showed an "expanding star" pattern by the name of Juliet. We tried to verify this information with several authorities on Dorflinger glass but failed. A dealer told us that a cutter said he remembered this pattern but couldn't recall at which company he'd cut it. He had worked for Dorflinger, Libbey, and several others.

563. A footed punch bowl in Alhambra by Meriden, but pattern also signed by Canadian companies. Roden Brothers named the pattern Norman.

564. A two-handled nappy signed by Gowans, Kent.

565. An 18-inch ice cream tray in #307-9 pattern by Roden Brothers.

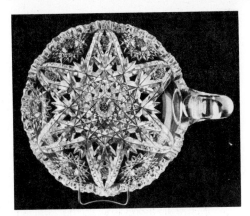

566. A handled nappy by an unidentified company.

567. A 14-inch tray by another unidentified company.

WRITERS

Several writers of cut glass books have given descriptive names to patterns they could not identify by catalog. When the catalog name became known, this caused confusion as to which to use. While a few people hesitate to give up the old descriptive name, most prefer the catalog identification.

RETAIL CATALOGS

Catalogs from retailers and wholesalers gave mostly secondary identification. When department or jewelry stores bought cut glass for retail trade, they often put out their own catalogs. Unfortunately most of them did not use the same name as the factory or cutting shop that produced the glass. Many only numbered rather than named the patterns. The retail store or wholesaler probably purchased the glass from small cutting shops that also did not name the pattern. These catalogs therefore illustrate many patterns you do not find in glass company's publications.

Marshall Field & Company even hired some glass companies, such as Fry and Parsche, to cut certain patterns exclusively for the store. These patterns appeared only in the Marshall Field catalog. Fry—perhaps others—cut glass for this department store under the pattern names of Owasco and Cayuga. A very popular pattern appeared only in a Marshall Field catalog for 1911–1912, under different numbers for the various shapes. In this pointed loops pattern, hobstars and cane filled the spaces in the background (568).

We have found other patterns only in the Marshall Field catalog, such as a comport with triple pointed ovals and hobstars, #70711 (569), and a saucer with hobstar dominance in #71433 (570). A catalog by G. W. Huntley pictured a bonbon with stars and notched miters as Hunter (571).

Knowing these altered and duplicated designs eliminates considerable confusion in the identification of catalog patterns. Those pieces with signatures settle any question of identification. Those without signatures narrow the identification to two or more companies.

568. A 13½-inch plate illustrated in the Marshall Field catalog.

569. A comport pictured in the Marshall Field catalog.

571. A bonbon identified by G. W. Huntley catalog for 1913 as Hunter.

570. A nappy identified by the Marshall Field catalog.

5

The Search for Identification

THE search to identify cut glass never ends. When you exhaust one source, you turn to another. You can identify cut glass by advertisements in old magazines, patent records, and signatures. Most research begins with a search for a signature. An identified signature provides the name of the company that produced the piece.

SIGNATURES

Toward the end of the nineteenth century, producers of cut glass decided that a signature offered a possible solution to the pirating of patented patterns. In 1895, Libbey and Hawkes took the lead and announced that they would place an acid-etched signature on all pieces of cut glass. In their magazine advertising they urged the customer to look for their trademark. Most of the other companies quickly followed the leaders and signed their glass with a patented signature. Several, such as Hoare, patented a trademark the company had used for several years.

To sign a piece of glass, the worker dipped a rubber stamp with a company trademark into an acid solution. Then he pressed the stamp against the glass to etch the signature.

LOCATION OF SIGNATURES

To locate a signature, hold the piece near a strong light and rotate it until you get a mirrorlike reflection. This reflection causes the signature to stand out. Knowing where to look simplifies the search. Most companies more or less standardized the location of signatures.

You'll find the inside center the most common location for a signature on any such piece as a bowl, nappy, or bonbon. If you don't find the signature there, then look on the edge of the base. Occasionally you will locate the signature on the inside of the top rim.

On footed pieces, companies put the signature on the top or botttom of the foot near the edge. For handled pieces, such as jugs, oils, sugar and cream, look on the flat at the top of the handle, under the handle, or on the base. On pieces with no foot, as tumblers, decanters, vases, check the edge of the base. Any item with a lid may have the signature on the inside center of one or both pieces.

When you fail to find a signature, search the unexpected places: on the lip of a jug, the neck of a carafe, the side of a miter, or the rim of a lid. Do not stop your search until you have checked every uncut surface on the item, then look again. You may find the signature in an odd place. Once you identify the signature, then try to find the pattern name.

A signed piece can lead to the identification of an unsigned one. A sugar and cream signed Clark led to the identification of a footed set that duplicated the pattern (572). A Dorflinger signature on the silver of a lamp provided the identity of a decanter in the same pattern (573).

We have seen a lamp with a Dorflinger signature in block letters, acid etched. After Christian Dorflinger died, the family decided to close the factory. In 1921, John Dorflinger, a relative, bought the blanks and operated a cutting shop and museum on the site of the old factory. He signed some of this glass with the block letter signature.

FORGERIES

With the growing importance given signatures, people began to forge them, especially the scripted ones: Fry, Clark, Irving, or Bergen. You can easily detect the work of an electric needle by scraping the signature with your

572. A footed sugar and cream signed Clark.

574. A 12-inch tray in Libbey pattern by Libbey but signed Fry.

573. A decanter cut in a Dorflinger pattern.

575. A celery on a figured blank with a Tuthill signature.

fingernail. Some forgers, fortunately, fail to research the authentic signature. Recently a man set up a booth at an antiques show in a shopping mall and offered to acid etch signatures on any piece of cut glass. He etched the Hawkes gravic glass signature on geometric patterns.

Knowing popular patterns can alert you to forgeries. A Libbey catalog identified this 12-inch tray as the Libbey pattern, but it has a Fry signature (574). In this case you naturally suspect forgery. The scripted Tuthill signature appears on this celery cut on a figured blank (575). We can only assume that someone forged the signature as the company did not use figured blanks.

UNIDENTIFIED SIGNATURES

From time to time collectors and dealers contact us about the identification of an unknown signature. We have not found any information on the following signatures. Two different collectors showed us jugs with M and A, each inside a C, all in block print (576). Two bowls with identical patterns display two different signatures: John W. Stots inside a wreath with a string bow and Ash Bros., both in block letters (577). A dealer wrote us about two clarets signed on the base of the foot, in block letters with the word ELLIS arranged in a semicircle.

A collector asked us to identify OMEGA signed with the E and A raised above the other letters. Another collector found J. W. H. in an oval on a nappy cut in Strawberry-Diamond and Flashed Fans. A celery contained PGC Co. enclosed in a shield. All these unknown signatures appear in the appendix. We would welcome any information on them.

In 1911, sixty-three representatives of thirty glass companies organized the National Association of Cut Glass Manufacturers to promote trade and preserve the quality of American cut glass. The association adopted a signature (see Appendix A). The number in the center identified the independent company. We could find no record that gave the number assigned to each company.

576. A jug with M and A enclosed in a C for a signature.

577. A 9-inch bowl signed John W. Stots and a matching one that has an Ash Bros. signature.

IDENTIFICATION BY SIGNATURE ONLY

We could not locate a large number of signed pieces in catalogs. This lack of identification indicates the gap in available catalogs.

Almy and Thomas. This cutting shop operated in Corning, New York, from 1903 to 1907. A vase with this signature alternated punties with notched miters and added a border of hobstars and fans (578).

Bergen. Two patterns by this company developed around intersecting pointed bars. One pattern utilized old motifs of crosshatching, nailhead diamond, and elongated hobstars in a simple design (579). The other pattern created an ornate design with flashed miters and hobstars (580).

Clark. A signed piece by this company used a lapidary center in the minor motif that united elongated 8-point stars (581). Intersecting bars with hobstar border characterized two patterns. Crosshatching covered the bars in one (582), and diamonds of crosshatching the other (583). A butter cover and plate contained rows of fans, a combination of crosshatching and single stars in squares, 8-point stars, and fans (584).

Two signed pieces by Clark illustrate the ornate and the simple in patterns. Hobstars completed the pattern in a heavily cut pointed loops outline (585). By contrast, a simply cut ash receiver let the hobstars form most of the pattern (586).

Four signed pieces by Clark combined the floral with geometrics. None of the available catalogs illustrate such patterns. Double bars of hobstars created spaces for the flowers in a low bowl (587). On a berry bowl, bars of cane framed the flowers (588). Another bowl set the flowers and leaves apart with bands of hobstars (589). A tumbler combined a flower with a raised star and geometrics (590). Probably a late Clark catalog would identify these pieces by pattern name.

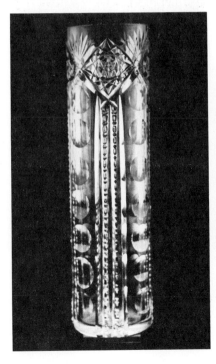

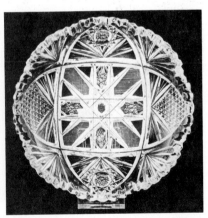

578. A vase with an Almy and Thomas signature.

579. A nappy signed Bergen.

580. A nappy bowl signed Bergen.

581. A 9-inch bowl signed Clark.

582. A 7-inch plate signed Clark.

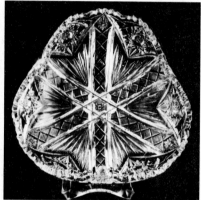

583. A bonbon signed Clark.

584. A butter cover and plate with a Clark signature.

585. A 9-inch bowl, heavily cut and signed Clark.

586. An ash receiver signed Clark.

587. A nappy bowl with a Clark signature.

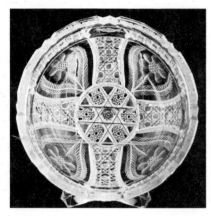

588. An 8-inch bowl signed by Clark.

589. An 8-inch bowl with a Clark signature.

590. A tumbler that has a Clark signature.

Egginton. A signed plate by Egginton placed a reverse fan in the points of the star outline, and hobstars filled the spaces between the points (591). A column of hobstars decorated a vase (592).

Fry. These two patterns illustrated Fry's top quality glass. Notched miters framed the hobstars on a bowl (593). Buzzstars served as the dominant motifs between the ornate pointed loops on this bonbon (594).

Hawkes. Several of the items signed by Hawkes demonstrate his typical style of cutting. A flower pot (595) and a candelabrum (596) used a hobstar border. The candelabrum also showed the webbed fan found on several patterns by Hawkes. In a typical pattern, a tobacco jar alternated a panel of hobstars with one of crosscut diamonds (597). Two other patterns relied strongly on older designs. A low bowl's pattern resembled the Gothic arch outline of Chrysanthemum (598), and the plate in border and miter suggested Marquis or Brunswick (599).

Five signed pieces exhibited diversity of miter outlines. Highly decorated bars and 8-point stars dominated a low bowl (600). Minute stars in pointed loops and thousand miter cutting created a design quite unlike Hawkes (601). Hobstars completed a complicated star outline on a bowl (602) and flat stars on a divided dish (603). A swirl pattern highlighted the double hobstars and crimp shape so characteristic of Hawkes (604). A diamond combination and fans joined the hobstars on this vase (605).

Hawkes created a novelty when he shaped a sugar and cream as cubes (606). A fancy dish in pointed loops and hobstars duplicated his crimp shapes (607). In a round tray, Hawkes combined pointed loops with a frame of Gothic arch and added panels of hobstars (608). A combination Gothic arch and star outline decorated a rectangular tray with hobstars (609). The catalog called a round plate with single stars within wreaths North Star (610).

591. A 12½-inch tray with an Egginton signature.

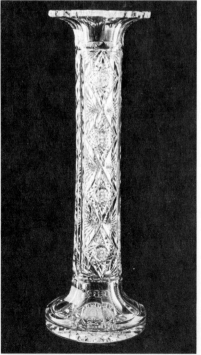

592. This vase has an Egginton signature.

593. A 9-inch berry bowl by Fry.

594. A bonbon with a Fry signature.

595. A flower pot by Hawkes.

596. A candelabrum signed Hawkes.

597. A tobacco jar with the Hawkes signature.

598. A low bowl similar to Chrysanthemum, signed Hawkes.

599. A 7½-inch plate in border and miter cut, signed Hawkes.

600. A low, crimped bowl with a Hawkes signature.

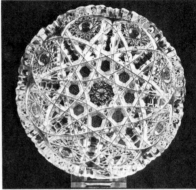

601. A 9-inch bowl signed Hawkes in a unique pattern.

602. A heavily cut low bowl with a Hawkes signature.

603. A bonbon with glass divider, signed Hawkes.

605. A vase in a unique shape with a signature by Hawkes.

604. A 10½-inch crimp bowl signed by Hawkes.

606. Only Hawkes cut this cube-shaped sugar and cream.

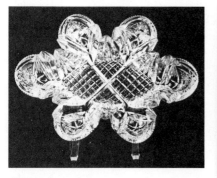

607. A fancy dish in crimp shape, signed by Hawkes.

608. A 14-inch plate signed by Hawkes.

609. Hawkes signed this rectangular tray.

610. A 14-inch plate signed by Hawkes, in North Star pattern.

To meet the competition, Hawkes combined flowers with geometric motifs. The flowers on a round tray with a geometric band (611) and those on a handled sandwich tray with buttons of cane strongly suggest the work of Sinclaire (612). Sinclaire possibly designed the fruit border for this plate (613), and the scene (614) at the time he worked with Hawkes.

Hoare. Hobstars served as the combination motif in a number of patterns by this company as indicated in the Corinthian type pattern shown here (615). A crimp low bowl in double pointed loops (616) emphasized Hoare's detailed cutting. A number of patterns by Hoare developed around crosshatched bars as in this lemonade or punch cup and saucer (617). Rows of fans, combination diamonds, and small double fans characterized a pattern on this plate (618). A flashed star dominated a signed, three-handled vase (619). A petaled hobstar on an oval bowl showed Hoare's creative ability (620).

Libbey. Most of Libbey's signed pieces showed ornate cutting. Deeply cut hobstars served as the dominant motif in a number of pieces. In a decanter, hobstars formed both the border around the base and the vertical panels (621). Two diamonds of crosshatching separated the hobstars on a jug (622). Hobstars completed the star outline on a low bowl (623). Three sizes of

611. A 10-inch plate that carries a Hawkes signature.

612. A handled sandwich plate signed Hawkes.

613. An 11½-inch plate with a Hawkes signature.

614. A 10-inch plate with a scene, signed Hawkes.

615. A 12-inch plate with a signature by Hoare.

616. A crimp, low bowl signed Hoare.

617. A lemonade or punch cup and saucer with a Hoare signature.

618. A 7-inch plate signed by Hoare.

619. A three-handled vase with a Hoare signature.

620. A 9-inch oval bowl signed by Hoare.

621. A decanter signed by Libbey.　　**622.** A jug in rare shape signed by Libbey.

623. Silver rims this low bowl with a Libbey signature.

hobstars decorated the swirls in a 10-inch bowl (624). Diamonds of small hobstars dominated the pattern on a signed under plate (625).

Hobstars decorated three different ice cream trays of Libbey. Hobstars and nailhead diamonds filled a center circle in an ice cream tray (626). An outline of intersecting circles required two sizes of hobstars on a tray (627). On a third tray intersecting circles and double pointed loops developed another pattern with small hobstars (628).

Three patterns on Libbey pieces strongly resembled other patterns of the company. Intersecting bars and flat stars in a low bowl looked similar to Leota (629). Flat stars and notched miters on a sugar resembled Ellsmere (630). A star outline and blocks suggested New Brilliant or Nassau (631).

One type of row outline differed considerably from Libbey's usual style of cutting. Rows of hobstars and lined rectangles formed the repetitive motifs on a nappy (632).

Libbey, along with Clark, cut the pinwheel in several patterns. The pattern on a jug combined a cluster of hobstars with a pinwheel (633). A pointed oval with nailhead diamonds and hobstar joined the pinwheels in a footed punch bowl (634).

624. A 10-inch low bowl with a swirl pattern and a Libbey signature.

625. An under plate, possibly to a jug, signed by Libbey.

626. An ice cream tray with a Libbey signature.

627. A 17½-inch tray signed by Libbey.

628. A 15½-inch oval tray with a Libbey signature.

630. A sugar in a pattern similar to Ellsmere with a Libbey signature.

629. A 10-inch low bowl similar to Leota and signed Libbey.

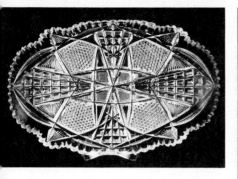

631. A tray in a pattern similar to Nassau and signed by Libbey.

632. A Libbey signature appears on this nappy.

633. Libbey signed this jug.

634. A footed punch bowl signed by Libbey.

Libbey followed the trend to combine motifs from nature with geometrics. Hobstars between the fan prongs and medallions of fruit characterized a pattern on an oval tray (635). Notched bars and flowers formed the pattern on an oval bowl (636). Minutely cut diamonds and rosettes created the border and encircled a hobstar on a round tray (637). Another tray repeated the same motifs around the hobstar but added medallions for flowers in the border (638). Odd flowers decorated the points of a nailhead star cut on a figured blank (639). Blazed stars and reversed fans formed the pattern on a vase (640).

Maple City. The signed pieces from this company exhibited excellent quality. Ornate intersecting bars and hobstars decorated this plate (641). Split squares and those of single stars formed the pattern on a hair receiver (642). Hobstars accented both the alternating circles and pointed loops of a pattern on a pickle tray (643). On a celery, pointed loops outlined the pattern with

636. An oval bowl signed by Libbey.

635. A 12-inch tray with a Libbey signature.

638. Libbey signed this 12-inch tray.

637. A 14-inch tray with a Libbey signature.

640. A late pattern in a vase signed by Libbey.

639. A bonbon with a Libbey signature.

641. A plate with a Maple City signature.

642. A hair receiver signed by Maple City.

643. A 6½-inch pickle tray with a Maple City signature.

644. A celery signed by Maple City.

ornate flashed fans and hobstars (644). A combination motif of cane and crosshatching united the hobstars on a vase (645). The foot of the comport pictured repeated the pinwheel on the bowl (646).

Parsche. Donald Parsche has stated that his father's company used a paper sticker most of the time. We found an acid-etched signature on a small plate with a border of hobstars and crosshatched buttons (647).

Pitkin & Brooks. A comport in Pitkin & Brooks quality alternated a shooting star with a hobstar (648).

Sinclaire. These signed items exhibited the strong Sinclaire characteristics previously mentioned. St. Louis diamonds surrounded a circle of hobstars (649). A leafy effect accented the hobstars on a jug (650). A border of hobstars and medallions circled a unique star in the center of one dish (651). Sinclaire placed this floral pattern alone on a jug and called it Pond Lilies, but we could not find a pattern name for this jug with the hobstar border and pond lilies (652).

Straus. Three signed pieces showed artistically cut patterns by Straus. A low bowl combined pointed loops and simulated circles against a background of cane (653). In this comport a combination of pointed ovals of crosshatching

645. A Maple City signature appears on this vase.

646. A comport with a Maple City signature.

647. A plate with the Parsche signature.

648. A comport signed by Pitkin & Brooks.

649. A 13½-inch tray signed by Sinclaire.

650. Sinclaire signed this jug.

651. A 9-inch dish with a Sinclaire signature.

652. A jug signed by Sinclaire.

653. A 10-inch low bowl signed by Straus.

and cane united the large hobstars (654). A Lackawanna Cut Glass catalog stated that the type of loving cup with a scalloped sawtooth rim actually served as a center vase. Intersecting bands of nailhead diamonds link the hobstars (655). One string box lined the miters (656), while the other notched them (657).

Two identical and distinctive shapes in jugs used hobstars as the dominant motif. We have only seen this unique shape in a jug with a Straus signature and pictured in a Straus magazine advertisement. On one jug, notched miters and crosscut diamonds joined a hobstar (658), while on the other a line of alternating single stars and hobstars performed this function (659). Both jugs contained cutting inside the neck.

Steuben. Although the Steuben Glass Works, 1903–1918, furnished blanks to Hawkes, Hoare, and a few others, it also cut glass. We found three signed pieces: a pinwheel motif on a decanter (660), a matching pair of pheasants (661), and a cologne in a rare shape (662).

654. A comport with the Straus signature.

655. A loving cup vase signed by Straus.

656. A string box with a Straus signature.

657. Straus signed this string box.

658. A jug signed by Straus.

659. A jug with a Straus signature.

660. A decanter signed by Steuben.

662. A cologne signed by Steuben.

661. A pair of pheasants with a Steuben signature.

Tuthill. The fact that we have never seen a Tuthill catalog explains the large number of patterns identified by signature only and not by name. Charles Tuthill produced and signed a number of geometric patterns. Without this signature you would not recognize such glass as Tuthill. Wallace Turner has stated that Tuthill furnished the formula for the blanks he ordered along with the shapes.

According to Turner, Tuthill cut only a limited number of pieces in the special design shown here. Turner owns a bowl and a 6-inch saucer in the pattern. The flashed hobstar in the center has crosshatched points. Circling this star you find rows of crosshatched buttons, 8-point stars, relief diamonds, and 8-point stars repeated. The border consists of fans and clear diamonds (663). A slightly similar pattern uses a crosshatched star in the center, and rows of single stars, relief diamonds, crosshatched buttons and 8-point stars (664). In Southern California we found a tray and matching jewel box in this ornate pattern. Needless to say, an item in this pattern adds exceptional value to any collection or inventory.

A hobstar comprised the dominant motif in a number of patterns as in this carafe (665). James and Susan Tuthill presented this as a wedding gift in 1904, according to the inscription. The signed vase for nasturtiums combined a large hobstar with crosshatching for the design (666).

A shell-shaped piece consisted of hobstars and pointed ovals (667). Crosshatched pointed ovals framed the minor motifs on this plate (668). A border of fine crosshatching circled the hobstars on a low bowl (669), the 8-point stars in this jug (670), and the medallions in a 10-inch plate (671). A reverse Gothic arch formed the outline for clusters of hobstars in this 8-inch bowl (672).

663. A 12-inch plate signed by Tuthill.

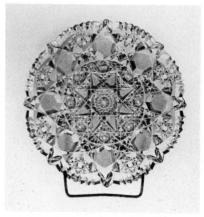

664. A 5-inch plate with a Tuthill signature.

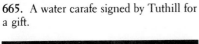

666. Tuthill signed this nasturtium vase.

665. A water carafe signed by Tuthill for a gift.

667. A shell bonbon signed by Tuthill.

668. A 7-inch plate with a Tuthill signature.

669. A low bowl signed by Tuthill.

670. A jug with a Tuthill signature.

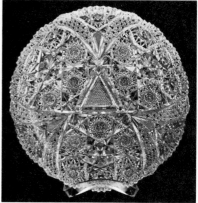

671. This 10-inch plate has a Tuthill signature.

672. An 8-inch bowl signed Tuthill.

Bars outlined a number of patterns. Notched miters framed the hobstars and the combination minor motifs on a plate (673). Hobstars completed the pattern on a crimp tray with an outline of curved bars (674). Curved bars of cane outlined the pattern on a low bowl (675).

Tuthill created several patterns with a pointed loops outline. On a crimp oval tray (676) and a round plate (677), hobstars dominated. A round tray contained flat stars and nailhead diamonds within the pointed loops (678). Beading outlined the pointed loops in an oval tray decorated with cane (679). Flashed fans accented the pointed loops of nailheads on a saucer (680).

Tuthill also cut other miter outlines. Two vases, one fan shape (681) and the other handled (682) placed hobstars in panels. A bowl used St. Louis diamonds to accent a heavily cut flashed star center (683). We found only one signed Tuthill piece with a pinwheel motif (684).

Tuthill also combined geometric cutting with motifs from nature. In a jewel box, 8-point stars joined flowers to form the design (685). Flat stars and blazed miters combined with a leafy border (686) on a sugar.

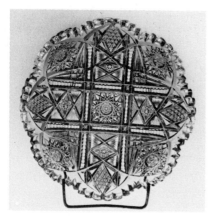

673. A 6-inch plate with a Tuthill signature.

674. A 14½-inch crimped tray signed by Tuthill.

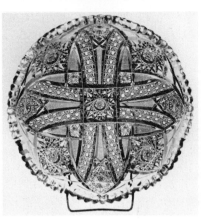

675. An 8-inch low bowl with a Tuthill signature.

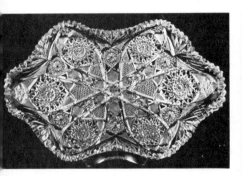

676. A crimp tray signed by Tuthill.

677. Tuthill signed this large plate.

678. An 8-inch tray with a Tuthill signature.

679. An 18-inch oval tray signed by Tuthill.

680. A saucer signed by Tuthill.

681. A fan-shaped vase with a Tuthill signature.

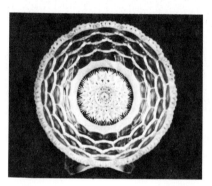

683. An 8½-inch bowl signed by Tuthill.

682. A two-handled vase signed by Tuthill.

685. Tuthill signed this jewel box.

684. An 8-inch bowl that has a Tuthill signature.

686. This sugar has a Tuthill signature.

687. A vase signed by Unger.

688. A 13½-inch tray signed by Unger.

689. An 8-inch bowl with a Wright signature.

Unger Brothers. Two pieces signed Unger Brothers illustrate the use of double fans to accent the combination motif on a vase with hobstars (687) and a rectangular tray with buzzstars (688).

Wright Rich Cut Glass Company. The bowl cut on a figured blank framed the flowers with pointed ovals of cane and crosshatching (689).

SIGNED CANADIAN GLASS

Within recent years more interest has developed in signed Canadian cut glass. We have seen one or more pieces of Canadian cut glass in several of the large collections we photographed.

Gundy-Clapperton. Pointed ovals complimented the hobstars on a nappy (690) and in a celery (691). Three miters framed the hobstars on a bowl (692). Unique row cutting characterized a flower basket (693).

Gowans, Kent. In a square bowl alternate rows of crosshatched buttons and of 8-point stars formed the pattern (694). Hobstars dominated a simple pattern on a jug (695). A decanter with a matching stopper and curved neck alternated a crosscut diamond with a combination of fan, crosshatched diamond and hobstar (696). This company produced a very high quality glass, difficult to distinguish from that made in the United States.

House of Birks. This company sold its glass factory to George Phillips & Company. When Mr. Phillips died, Mrs. Phillips managed the company. Many of the signed pieces have a combination signature of Birks and the distributor. We did find a vase in hobstars and crosshatched diamonds with only the Birks signature (697).

Roden Brothers. This company cut both quality and a poor grade of glass. A pattern on a bowl consisted of a star outline and hobstars (698).

691. A celery with the Gundy-Clapperton signature.

690. A nappy signed by Gundy-Clapperton.

693. A Gundy-Clapperton signature appears on this flower basket.

692. A 9½-inch bowl with Gundy-Clapperton signature.

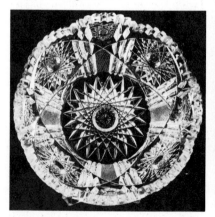

694. A square bowl signed by Gowans, Kent.

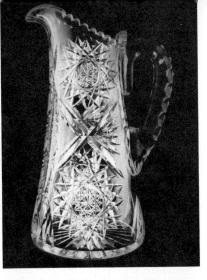

695. A jug with the Gowans, Kent signature.

697. A vase with a Birks signature.

696. A decanter signed by Gowans, Kent.

698. An 8-inch bowl signed by Roden Brothers.

IDENTIFICATION BY PATENT RECORDS

Companies patented a pattern to protect it from theft by other firms. In regard to the Heart pattern, Pitkin & Brooks stated in a 1907 catalog, "The copying of our new patterns by glass manufacturers in the past, caused us, this year to protect ourselves on this pattern by securing Letters Patent." A number of other companies followed the same procedure. The letters patent contained a sketch of one section of the pattern. You can find this sketch in a volume of patent records.

When anyone mentions searching patent records to identify cut glass, you may throw up your hands in despair. Who wants to make a special trip to the patent office in Washington, D.C., and go through musty old volumes? But you can find them much closer. A collector in San Francisco made a trip to the capitol to examine the patent records for glass vessels and learned that he could have found a duplicate set at the patent library only thirty miles south of his home. Large public libraries often have these volumes of patent records.

Some collectors who do look at patent records get upset when they discover that the pattern name does not appear with the sketch. Hawkes frequently named the pattern in his letters patent, but most companies did not. The records do give the date, the name of the designer, the company to which he assigned the patent, and a sketch of the pattern.

Rather than give a pattern a descriptive name, we prefer to list the date of the patent and the company that applied for it.

AMERICAN CUT GLASS COMPANY

This company operated in Chicago from 1896 to 1914 as a branch of Libbey. W. C. Anderson secured patents on two hobstar patterns. The January 19, 1904, #36739 pattern joined the hobstars with flashed stars (699). Feathered fans united the hobstars in #36865, April 5, 1904 (700). This second pattern someone has described as "Mary."

699. A nappy patented by American Cut Glass Company.

700. A punch bowl with a patent by American.

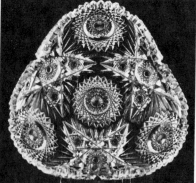

CLARK

Patent #32150, January 30, 1900, featured the lapidary center in the major motif for a star outline (701).

701. A 9½-inch low bowl patented by Clark.

GIBBS, KELLEY & COMPANY

This company, located in Honesdale, Pennyslvania, from 1880 to 1905, patented a pattern on November 7, 1899, #31781. William Henry Gibbs designed the bowl with hobstars in circles and cane with nailheads on the button (702).

702. A 9-inch bowl Gibbs, Kelley & Company patented.

MERIDEN

William R. Elliot received a patent for two patterns assigned to this company that operated in Meriden, Connecticut, from 1895 to 1923. A jug in #32210, February 13, 1900, used five different motifs to accent hobstars (703). Cane diamonds and short miters linked hobstars on the border with the one in the center of this bowl, #32211, February 13, 1900 (704).

703. A jug with a Meriden patent.

704. Meriden patented this bowl.

STRAUS

Herman Richmond patented design #35323 on November 26, 1901. You may have heard this pattern described as "drape" (705). Benjamin Davies applied for the patent #81788 granted on October 31, 1899. In this bowl single stars accented the alternating regular and reverse Gothic arches (706). Someone also called this pattern "planeta."

705. Herman Richmond patented the design on this bowl for Straus.

706. Straus patented this design on an 8-inch bowl.

IDENTIFICATION BY MAGAZINE ADVERTISEMENTS

Public and private libraries have issues of old magazines, but you may need special permission to examine them. Prepare to spend hours flipping through the pages to find cut glass advertisements. Or you may meet a collector of old magazines who will permit you to study them. A number of the major companies advertised in such magazines as *Glass & Crockery Journal*, *Harper's* magazine, *Cosmopolitan*, *McClure's*, *Scribner's*, *Century*, and *Ladies' Home Journal*. You can possibly find others. Occasionally the company did not provide a catalog name or number with the picture. Even without such identification of pattern, you can at least attribute the design to the company that produced it.

This Bergen advertisement mentioned the "new 80-page, handsomely illustrated 1907 catalogue . . ." (707). Fry listed Winner as the name of a punch bowl (708). He called another pattern Venetian in this advertisement. and Clark identified the Snowball pattern (709). We matched this tobacco jar to a Dorflinger advertisement in *Scribner's*, February, 1897 (710).

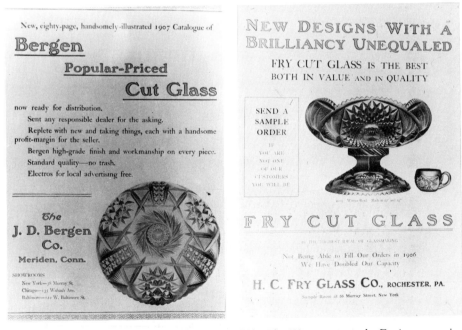

707. A magazine advertisement by Bergen.

708. The Winner pattern by Fry in a magazine advertisement.

710. A Dorflinger advertisement pictured the pattern on this tobacco jar.

709. Venetian by Fry and Snowball by Clark in a double magazine advertisement.

Hawkes usually named the advertised patterns, such as Constellation, but Rochester Cut Glass Company, associated with Fry, only gave a number, 143 and 114 (711). Hawkes named the pattern on the vase Alice in this advertisement (712). Wright identified this footed punch bowl with hobstar dominance and pointed ovals as Mercedes (713).

Oddly enough we identified one pattern by the butterfly cut, by Thomas Mortensen for the Niland Cut Glass Company of Meriden, Connecticut (714).

While signatures and patent records do give positive identification as to the company, they do not provide the same satisfaction that comes with knowing the pattern name given in a catalog or advertisement. Signatures require less time spent in a careful search of the piece and recognition of the trademark. Patent records and magazine advertisements require hours of searching for glass vessels or cut glass, unless you rely on the research of someone else. Perhaps the future will uncover more old catalogs to provide elusive pattern names to match signatures, patent records, or nonidentifying advertisements.

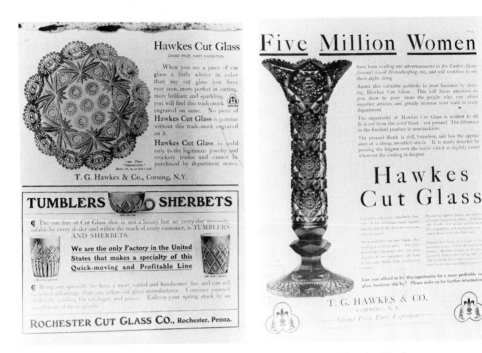

711. Constellation by Hawkes and 143 and 114 by Rochester in a double advertisement.

712. A vase in Alice by Hawkes.

713. A footed punch bowl in Mercedes by Wright.

714. A comport by Niland with the Mortensen butterfly.

6

Innovations in Cut Glass

WHEN the demand for cut glass waned from time to time, companies resorted to different methods to stimulate buying. Two innovations came early in the Brilliant Period: adding color to the crystal blank and trimming the glass with silver. These decorative touches did not necessarily change the geometric patterns.

The third innovation, engraving with stone and copper wheels, did depart from the old geometric patterns. Engraving, an ancient art, demanded more skill than cutting. While American companies always did some engraving, Tuthill and Sinclaire popularized it during the Brilliant Period.

COLORED CUT GLASS

Identified patterns by catalogs indicated the following companies produced colored glass: Bergen, Clark, Dorflinger, Fry, Libbey, Hawkes, Hoare, Mt. Washington, and Boston and Sandwich Glass Company. Pairpoint produced much of the colored glass in the 1920s. No doubt other companies produced colored cut glass, but none except Hawkes listed it in their catalogs. A Hawkes catalog offered a dinner bell, clarets, and a roemer in ruby or green. Roemer describes a drinking glass with a hollow cylindrical stem and an ovoid bowl. With so little information available, these facts may help you in recognizing and buying American colored cut glass.

PROCESS

These companies cut designs on both solid and color-cut-to-clear. The color-cut-to-clear glass consisted of a colored layer placed over the crystal blank. If you look along an edge you can see where the line of color joined the clear glass in this overlay method. Americans use *overlay* as a synonym for *cased glass*.

Much of the new color-cut-to-clear glass from Europe flashed the color.

Flashing denotes a much thinner layer of glass that easily wore away, a thin coating of a different color.

COLORS

The primary shades of ruby, green, blue, and amber will help you distinguish American from European glass. In American glass, ruby and green dominate the number of pieces in color-cut-to-clear. From batch to batch, the metal for overlaying varied slightly in color. The red ranged from ruby to cranberry. Amber sometimes came out apricot. The medium green may shade into a turquoise or aqua. Several colors formed a rainbow piece.

European glass differs from American in the color tones. The English cranberry looks lighter than that of the American, and the Bohemian Ruby has a very dark red tone. The Bohemians used a dark green instead of the medium shade of American glass. American blue seems almost a bright navy when compared to the royal of the Bohemians. We have seen European glass in red-cut-to-gold and in red-and-gold-cut-to-clear. So far, we cannot authenticate these color combinations as produced by American companies.

Even experts have difficulty distinguishing some American from European colored glass. Study the color in positively identified pieces of American and European glass so as to develop a "feel" for the different shades.

Solid colors in American glass included red, blue, green, and amber. The ruby and blue appear in the same tones as color-cut-to-clear. Hoare used rose for several solid colored pieces. The amber looks quite dark. Unfortunately the camera does not exactly reproduce the color tone, so you'll want to study actual pieces at every opportunity. Glass done in color-cut-to-clear apparently outnumbered the solid colored pieces cut in geometric patterns of the Brilliant Period.

PATTERNS

A number of companies produced color-cut-to-clear glass in such patterns as Block, Hob Diamonds, Flutes, Strawberry-Diamond, and Russian. As with the crystal glass, identifying the company proves an almost impossible task in regard to these patterns.

A number of companies copied their own popular patterns for colored glass. By identifying the pattern by catalog or patent record, in most instances you can verify the company that produced the piece. Dorflinger not only produced the blanks but did considerable cutting in color. He produced the following patterns in color: Montrose, Hob Diamond, and Hob and Lace (232), Renaissance (531), #28 (236), Parisian (239), Marlboro (66), Prism, and a vase similar to Libbey's Harvard (519). Several patterns cut by Dorflinger in color have not been identified by name.

At the Wayne County Historical Museum in Honesdale we saw a piece of clear cut glass with delicate, bluish-purple flowers. Supposedly the artisan threw away the notes on the process when Mr. Dorflinger made fun of the product.

At this same museum in Honesdale, we saw a piece in a champagne color. According to one story Dorflinger put a fifty dollar gold coin in the batch of clear glass to produce this color. A person who had worked for the company said she saw him toss in the coin. A man whose father also worked for Dorflinger commented, "He probably palmed the coin as he loved doing magic tricks. Besides, he was rather tight with his money." Furthermore, a gold coin would not affect the metal; only an oxide would blend with the batch.

A short time later a collector showed us a low bowl in this same champagne color or pale amber. The pattern on this bowl matched Du Barry in a Quaker City catalog (715). We have found no record showing this company cut colored glass. It did rename patterns in public domain. In another puzzle, a cranberry vase cut in punties and miters motif duplicated pattern #634 illustrated in a Pitkin & Brooks catalog. We have found no other colored pieces cut by this company.

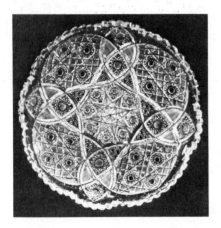

715. An 11-inch plate in Du Barry by Quaker City, identified by catalog.

Hawkes cut several of his patterns in color. These patterns include Venetian (269), Brazilian, Grecian (123), Gladys (521), Strawberry-Diamond and Fan (270), Flute and Prism, and Chrysanthemum (494). Color pieces by Hoare seem slightly fewer in number, but you can find then in such patterns as Monarch (547), Acme (321), and Croesus (323). We have seen a blue cut-to-cranberry loving cup in Crystal City by Hoare, very rare (326).

Other companies either did not cut as much color as these three or else they did not use identified patterns. Mt. Washington cut Wheeler (368) in color. Libbey reproduced such patterns in color as Harvard (518) and Prism. A bowl in Ruby cut-to-clear matched a Bergen pattern identified by patent record #27457 dated June 21, 1897. You may have heard the pattern described as "dauntless" which we could not authenticate. Shortly before the Boston and Sandwich Glass Company went out of business, it tried to recoup financially by producing colored and color-cut-to-clear cut glass.

The Empire Cut Glass Company experimented with a new type of colored glass. Some pieces added amber or blue handles and a matching base to a sugar and cream, basket, and nappy. A blue bowl may have an amber base or rim. A very rare bowl consisted of half amber and half blue with neither color milking into the other. Louis Iorio cut all of these bowls in the Success pattern (716). Any collector owning any of these pieces has a rare treasure.

These patterns merely indicate the pieces we have seen and identified by pattern name and do not by any means include all patterns produced in color. These you must identify by American motifs.

716. A two-handled nappy bowl in Success pattern by Empire, the design used for experimental colored glass.

MOTIFS

We showed Thomas Matthews a cigarette lighter we bought hoping he could give us some information about it. Matthews is a third-generation cutter and engraver. When he immediately identified the piece as American, we asked him why. He said that Americans cut the pointed miter deeper and narrower than the Europeans. The Americans dressed the pointed stone wheels to an angle of approximately 65 degrees, which they needed to do frequently. These deep miters of the Americans needed a heavier blank and more time and effort spent on polishing. The difficulty and time necessary to hand polish these deep cuts may have encouraged the discovery and use of acid polish.

The Europeans cut a shallower and wider pointed miter that they could put on a lighter blank and which polished easily by hand. When the Europeans dressed their stone wheels, they tried for a 90- to 100-degree angle. This technical difference in the pointed miter angle may help you distinguish between American and European glass.

The type of motif will separate American colored glass from imported. Look for the 8-point star, hobstars, notched prisms, or full pinwheels. While Americans cut punties and cane, these usually accented the dominant motif. Only Americans crosscut the diamond. In fact most of the American motifs contained more detailed cutting than those on imported glass. Study your American motifs so that you can easily recognize them.

Rumors often spread among dealers and collectors of cut glass. One such rumor related that present-day cutters, upon request, have given more detail cutting to the motifs on imported overlay glass. In making them more ornate, the pieces would more nearly resemble ones cut in the United States. Whether this rumor—defintely a rumor—has any truth or not, do verify the pattern, the motifs, the shade of color, and the shape as American.

SHAPES

You can learn to recognize American shapes. The jugs, comports, carafes, decanters, and vases follow certain traditional shapes as pictured in this book. In fact any piece in color that repeated a shape in clear glass possibly identifies it as American. Occasionally exceptions do occur, and then you must rely on other means of identification, such as motif or pattern.

By all means check the motifs on such popular shapes as bowls, punch bowls, bonbons, trays, and plates. The shapes on these vary little from their European counterparts.

SIGNATURES

Very little colored glass has a signature. We have seen Hawkes signed on a Strawberry-Diamond and Fan wine glass and a ruby decanter in Chrysanthemum. Clark signed a green punch cup and saucer and a decanter in Flute. A blue water carafe had a Fry signature.

A new source of worry has developed over color-cut-to-clear glass. A November 2, 1978, *Newsweek* article pictured ornate geometric designs in color-cut-to-clear produced in Talien, China, where craftsmen received $30 for a forty-eight hour week. We have seen three such items, only one of which contained a Chinese signature. They closely resembled American glass in their motifs and patterns.

Study the shape and quality of the blank, the patterns and motifs of the piece, the quality and detail of the pattern, and the shade of color. Then when you buy colored glass, be knowledgeable but beware.

SILVER

Silver enriched cut glass regardless of whether sterling or plate. Meriden identified its silver as quadruple plate. Silver plate adorned as much quality cut glass as did sterling. The type of silver depended on the company and the cost.

HALLMARKS

Several cut glass companies produced their own silver and signed it with their hallmark: Pairpoint, Dorflinger, Hawkes, Meriden (later International

Silver), and Unger. Most companies only cut the glass and then Tiffany & Company, Inc., Gorham Corporation, House of Birks, Shreve & Company, or other companies added the silver. Silver on unidentified patterns provided only the name of the silver company and not the firm that produced the glass. Unless the hallmark belonged to a glass company, it offers very little help in identifying who cut the glass.

SHAPES

The catalogs illustrated certain groups of items with silver. Silver tops covered salt and pepper sets (717), ink bottles, mucilage pots (718), and dresser jars. You'll find silver caps or stoppers on bitters bottles (719), colognes (720), and demijohns (721). A syrup (722) or honey pot (723) used a silver lid as did tobacco and cracker jars. Silver connected the two parts of hinged boxes: glove (724), handkerchief (725), jewel (726), and puff (727).

717. Salt and pepper in Alberta by Hawkes, 1905 catalog.

718. Mucilage pot with silver top.

719. A bitters bottle in Russian with silver top.

720. A cologne with an ornate silver stopper.

721. A demijohn in Suffolk by Hawkes has a silver stopper.

722. A syrup with a typical silver top.

723. A honey pot with a cut out for the server.

724. A glove box with silver fittings.

725. Silver fittings adorn this handkerchief box.

726. Silver fittings appear on this jewel box signed Fry.

727. A puff box with silver fittings.

A number of items trimmed with silver did not appear in the catalogs, such as the large jug shown here (728), but lamps and a candelabrum which contained silver fittings (729) did. Companies added silver to protect the rims of plates (730), bowls (731), and punch bowls (732). A number of vases (733) and comports (734) contained silver rims.

While relatively rare, silver did form a foot or base of a comport (735). At a lecture we gave, a woman showed us a jug in Brunswick by Hawkes with a silver base. Another collector owned a rare rose globe with both a rim and foot in silver (736).

Cut glass handles went on such silver items as a punch ladle, ice cream knife, berry spoon, and salad fork and spoon. Pairpoint made medal holders for vases, cigarette holders, and similar items. No doubt you can find other pieces decorated with silver.

728. A jug with a silver neck.

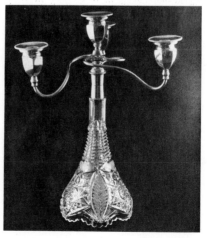

729. A candelabrum with silver fittings for candles.

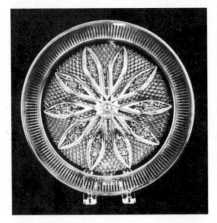

730. A silver rim on a plate with pointed loops outline.

731. A plain rim on an 8-inch low bowl.

732. An ornate rim on a punch bowl.

733. A vase with a silver rim in Boston by Pairpoint, identification by catalog.

734. A comport with a silver rim.

735. A comport with a silver foot.

736. A rose globe with both a silver rim and foot.

DESIGN

The type of design on the silver varied with the shape and the pattern. Jugs (737) and punch bowls often contained clusters of grapes on the band. A heavily cut piece might use a contrasting plain band, or a simple pattern contain an ornate one. Flowers and scrolls frequently decorated the ornate band (738).

The width of the silver depended upon the piece, its shape, and pattern. In fact the widths varied so widely on the same shape that we could not set up basic measurements.

From time to time, the addition of silver has hidden a broken or chipped rim or foot. Knowing the pieces decorated with silver and the type of decoration will help you recognize these additions. The addition often does not show the same quality of workmanship as that done originally by the factory. The foot or band may look out of balance with the rest of the shape or seem loose.

737. A jug with a grape design on the silver.

738. A 14½-inch tray with ornate silver rim in Daisy by Mt. Washington.

DESIGN FROM NATURE

When the consumer grew tired of the old geometric patterns, a number of companies turned to engraving flowers, fruits, birds, and scenes. Because flowers dominated the designs, most people refer to these years as the Flower Period.

The engraved designs consisted of two types: stone and copper wheel or a combination of the two. In intaglio, the engraver worked looking through the blank with the glass between him and the wheel. The engraver sculptured out the design—the reverse of cameo—with the stone wheel and did not completely polish out the whiteness on the glass created by the engraving. In copper wheel, the engraver brought the glass up to the wheel, locating it between him and the item. To make rock crystal the craftsman completely polished the engraving. Most of the major companies did one or both of these types of engraving.

HAWKES

Hawkes referred to his intaglio pieces as *gravic glass* and identified them with a special signature. The gravic glass took the name of flowers, such as Carnation (739), Chrysanthemum (740), Thistle (741), Poppy (742), and Iris (743). In the 1950s he cut the same flowers on thinner glass and named them Satin Iris or Satin Carnation. The thickness of the blank will indicate the early or late pieces.

Hawkes also cut fruit, such as Strawberry (744). His rock crystal products became more popular after the 1920s.

739. A footed punch bowl in gravic glass, Carnation pattern, signed Hawkes.

740. A jug in Chrysanthemum gravic glass signed Hawkes.

41. A comport in Thistle signed Hawkes.

742. A decanter in Poppy signed Hawkes.

743. A jug in Iris, signed with gravic glass signature by Hawkes.

744. A large plate in Strawberry, gravic glass, and signed Hawkes.

Late in the Brilliant Period Libbey cut some flowers. The catalogs illustrated Rose (745) and Poppy (746). A signature identified a stylized flower (747) and two unidentified flowers (748 and 749). Libbey also cut fruit in Cherry Blossom (750) and Cherry (751). Wisteria, sometimes called "Love Birds," became the best-known pattern of this type (752).

745. A jug in Rose pattern signed Libbey.

746. A jug signed Libbey in Poppy.

747. A stylized flower on an 8-inch bowl signed Libbey.

748. An unidentified flower on a jug signed by Libbey.

749. An unidentified flower on a 10-inch plate signed Libbey.

750. A low bowl in Cherry Blossom by Libbey.

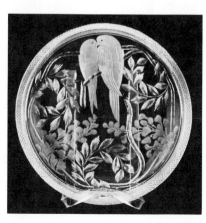

751. A jug signed Libbey in Cherry pattern.

752. An 8-inch low bowl in Wisteria by Libbey.

A Pairpoint catalog illustrated three patterns with veined leaves but different flowers: Arbutus (753), Anemone (754), and Murillo (755). Two patterns honored the daisy: Butterfly and Daisy (756) and Daisy (757).

753. A jug and tumbler in Arbutus by Pairpoint.

754. A flower center by Pairpoint in Anemone.

755. A punch bowl in Murillo by Pairpoint.

757. A clock in Daisy by Pairpoint.

756. A 13½-inch flower holder in Butterfly and Daisy by Pairpoint.

SINCLAIRE

As a naturalist, Sinclaire developed his patterns around nature. While collectors own a number of his geometrics and the combinations of geometric and engraving, very few showed us examples of floral only, as in R. C. Arctotis (758).

758. A whiskey jug with matching stopper in R. C. Arctotis by Sinclaire.

STRAUS

A patent record of October 24, 1916, #49807, identified this pattern with the rather unusual bird as cut by Herman Richman for Straus (759).

759. A punch bowl, patent number #49807 by Straus.

TUTHILL

The name of the flower or fruit identified the patterns by Tuthill, who continued to favor the rose as he engraved several varieties: Silver Rose (760), Evening Primrose (761), and Cut Rose (762). Mortensen's Butterfly and Flower decorated the lamp (763).

A number of patterns emphasized other flowers: Morning Glory (764), Wood Lily (765), Field Iris (766), Lilliaceae (767), and Daisy (768). The patterns in Rosemere (769), Phlox (770), and Nasturtium (771) gave the leaves as much importance as the flower.

Tuthill engraved several patterns depicting fruit. Strawberry Blossom contained the fruit, leaves, bud, and blossom (772). A pattern included all the fruits in the name: Orange, Pears, Grapes, and Cherries (773). A similar fruit pattern went by the name of Grapes, Cherries, and Pears (774).

In summary, while all cut glass has risen in value, colored and intaglio have increased far more than the clear geometric pieces.

760. A 10-inch plate in Silver Rose by Tuthill.

761. A comport or sweet pea vase by Tuthill in Evening Primrose.

762. A pickle dish or spoon tray in Cut Rose b‍ Tuthill.

763. A lamp in Mortensen's Butterfly and Flower, from Tuthill.

764. Morning Glory by Tuthill in a comport.

765. A comport in Wood Lily by Tuthill.

766. Field Iris by Tuthill in a vase.

768. A teapot in Daisy by Tuthill.

767. Lilliaceae, the name of the design on this vase by Tuthill.

769. A 10-inch plate in Rosemere by Tuthill.

770. A 10-inch plate in Phlox by Tuthill.

771. A low bowl in Nasturtium by Tuthill.

773. A dish in Orange, Pears, Grapes, and Cherries by Tuthill.

772. Tuthill low bowl in Strawberry Blossom.

774. A 12-inch plate in Grapes, Cherries, and Pears by Tuthill.

7

Unidentified Treasures

IN many of the collections we photographed, we found some beautiful—even exceptional—pieces for which we could secure no identification. This resulted from two basic situations.

First, the many small shops that cut glass contributed to the lack of identification. While much of their work included adaptations of popular patterns or cutting those no longer protected by patent, common sense tells you that they must have created some outstanding patterns from time to time. Again, we cannot document this.

Second, lack of identification also results from gaps in the chronology of available catalogs that illustrated cut glass patterns. At the time of publication, people did not consider the catalogs worth saving. Fortunately in every generation we find hoarders. We need to do more to locate and preserve any material about brilliant cut glass.

Never hesitate to buy an outstanding piece of cut glass with no identification, or you could miss a super buy. Instead learn how to look for the factors that add value to a piece of cut glass. A number of different characteristics make an item outstanding. Most of the pieces in the following illustrations show several of these characteristics. The more of them a piece of cut glass shows, the greater its value. In the final analysis, you must make the decision of whether or not to buy. Perhaps these suggestions will help you recognize exceptional value in unidentified treasures.

SYMMETRY IN PATTERN

Symmetry ranks as a prime prerequisite of quality glass. Symmetrical patterns exhibit a strong miter outline. The outline may vary from simple swirl (775) to a uniquely cut pointed loops (776). Certainly you want to look for an unusual interpretation of a basic miter outline, as in this tray where the designer gave a unique curve to the basic star outline (777).

A pattern generally contained repetitive segments within the miter outline.

775. A 9½-inch low bowl in a swirl outline in symmetrical cut.

776. A leaf-shaped, large tray with excellent symmetry.

777. A 17-inch tray with a unique star outline.

The number of segments depended on the size and the shape of the piece.
These divisions of the pattern should exactly duplicate each other. In the bowl
pictured here you will find this balance in segments of hobstars and bands of
cane (778). When the designer worked with an odd number of segments or
overlapped them, the symmetry became more difficult as in this crimped bowl
(779). Train your eyes to search for such duplication and balance.

Although a piece has a strong outline and duplicates repetitive segments, it
also needs to blend the motifs. In this ice cream tray, the cane motif of the
background perfectly accented the pointed ovals of nailhead diamonds and
hobstars on either side of the Gothic arches (780). In a more ornate pattern,
flashed fans softened the star points so they blend better with the pinwheels
and hobstars (781).

When you check a piece for symmetry, look for a strong miter outline,
duplication of segments, and blending of motifs in a pattern.

778. A 10-inch bowl with precision in segments.

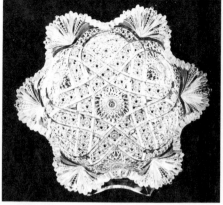

779. A crimp bowl with overlapping segments.

780. An 18-inch tray with an excellent blend of motifs.

781. A 9½-inch berry bowl with a soft blend of motifs.

DETAIL CUTTING

An outstanding piece should show exceptional detail and sharpness in cutting, both to the eye and to the touch. An item does not need an elaborate cutting to meet this qualification, as in this footed bonbon where crosshatched diamonds dominate the detailed pattern (782).

Sharp and minute cutting does provide a prismatic beauty, as seen in this footed decanter with matching stopper, both in a diamond cut (783). The shape and cutting on the foot and the unique handles add to its value. A tray in a 5-point star and clear button illustrates another type of minute cutting, more difficult than that of the decanter because of the more complicated motif (784). The star outline of this heavily cut bowl used a double ring of hobstars to complete the pattern (785).

Detailed and sharp cutting shows much better on a large item and attracts more attention, but don't overlook a well-cut, small piece.

782. A covered and footed bonbon with detailed cutting.

783. Sharp diamond cutting on a decanter with unique handle and foot.

784. An 11½-inch tray with detailed cutting.

785. A detailed cutting on an 8-inch bowl.

MAGIC IN MOTIFS

Many designs in cut glass followed certain traditional forms in which a hobstar or pinwheel formed the dominant motif. Cane, crosscut diamonds, crosshatching, or fans—to name a few—accented the dominant motif.

In a quality piece, the designer possibly started with a basic miter cut. From there on his imagination took over, and he visualized more artistic applications of old motifs. In this jug, vertical miters formed a base for the interlocking circles of single stars, but horizontal miters created the border (786).

Two small plates illustrate the effective use of motifs. The strong miter cut of double loops projected strength, but the simple decorations fired the imagination (787). Sinclaire might have created this swirling image accented with "moons" and "stars" (788).

Application of new interpretations to old motifs added magic. The decorated, intersecting miters within the circle united by bars of hobstars immediately set this bowl apart as an unusual use of motifs (789). The extreme precision of the panels and circles made this tray an outstanding piece (790). In this cake tray, the clear spot where the foot joined the plate formed the center of the hobstar. Nailhead diamonds and a border of hobstars and crosshatched diamonds completed the pattern (791). Whenever the designer saw magic in motifs, he created unique patterns.

787. An 8-inch plate with an interesting use of old motifs.

786. A jug that illustrates creative use of old motifs.

788. A 7-inch plate with a swirl and accenting "moons" and "stars."

789. A new creation of intersecting miters in an 8-inch bowl.

790. An extreme precision of motif in a square plate.

791. A cake tray with unique and detailed cutting, especially in the center star.

EXTRA FEATURES

Many of these unidentified treasures contain extra features. Begin with the basic shape of a piece and then compare this to the quality piece. A celery ordinarily does not have a foot, but this one has a tall one and a heavily cut pattern of hobstars and nailhead diamonds (792). Note the hobstar on the base of the foot. The low foot and the shape of this well-cut jug made it unique (793).

The addition of a lid or a holder to a piece that normally contained none indicates quality. This large bowl in Gothic arch and hobstars had a tight-fitting lid and an unusual shape (794). The silver base with applied handles and the lid with matching cut glass finial made this piece extremely rare (795). We have heard these shapes described as "Tom and Jerry" bowls or syllabubs, possibly later terms. The available catalogs do not picture these shapes.

Companies produced large numbers of celery trays but not as many upright ones. This celery in a row outline contained the extra feature of two handles (796). The shape of the handles and the cutting provided additional value. It also illustrated symmetry and detail in cutting.

While companies also cut decanters in abundance, shape and extra features made the difference in value. The different shape, the blend of the cutting with the shape, and the matching stopper set this decanter apart from others (797). Another decanter has a detailed pattern, heavily notched flutes on the neck, and a matched neck ring. The stopper matched the pattern on the decanter even to the notched neck (798).

792. A footed celery with detailed cutting.

793. A footed jug with an odd shape.

794. A covered punch bowl.

796. A celery in a row outline and handles cut with hobnails.

795. A covered punch bowl on a silver stand.

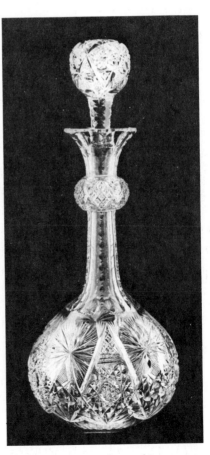

797. An artistically cut decanter in a rare shape, and matching stopper.

798. A decanter with matching stopper and neck ring.

UNIQUE SHAPES

The unique shape of an item indicated originality, a willingness to try something more artistic. Again you must first think in terms of the popular shapes and then compare them to the one under scrutiny. Most jugs followed standard shapes, but not all. This jug deviated from the standard with a bulge in the center and a low placement of the decorated handle (799). We found this shape but not the pattern in an Empire catalog, suggesting an innovative shape by Fry. Another jug with a very rare shape provided contrast in the heavily cut lower part and the plain neck (800).

Do remember that unique shapes generally demanded special patterns. Two vases more than meet this qualification. The scalloped foot and bulging shape make this vase unique (801). Another vase has such outstanding features as shape, square base on foot, ornate design, and repetitive pattern on the neck (802). This well-cut, cornucopia vase illustrated the extra features of shape, hobstar cut base and knob stem on foot, and step cutting on the pointed end (803). A shower vase, according to a catalog, showed a very simple pattern that contrasted the unique shape (804). Most unique shapes exhibit other characteristics already mentioned.

800. A jug with a heavily cut base and plain neck.

799. An odd-shaped jug with a low-placed handle.

801. A bulging vase with a scalloped foot.

802. A tall vase with repetitive pattern on the neck.

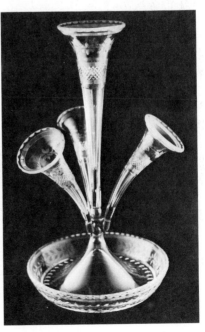

803. A cornucopia vase.

804. A shower vase in a simple pattern.

ODDITIES

An oddity means one or two of a kind. Gifts or presentation pieces created many such oddities. Some of these gave the name and date of the presentation. Other oddities resulted from craftsmen using leftover metal to make whimseys. Someone probably cut this pestle and mortar in Russian for a druggist (805). The decanter in the shape of a barrel with a spigot and small bucket would delight any collector (806). The round tray with the eagle contained thirteen hobstars, "moons," and single "stars," symbolizing the original colonies (807). Other oddities include a baseball bat, a bowling pin decanter, and a club for a policeman.

805. A pestle and mortar in Russian.

806. A barrel decanter with spigot and bucket of silver.

807. A 15-inch tray with an eagle, "moons," and "stars" representing the thirteen colonies.

RARITY

Bowls, nappies, tumblers, carafes, and jugs the companies created by the hundreds, but special items they produced only in limited numbers. You may see these pieces occasionally and even own one. Coffee and tea pots appeared in limited numbers. On this distinctive pot note the ornate cluster pattern, the cut handle, the delicate shape of the spout, and the decoration on the lid (808). The shape of the lid, the decorated spout, and simple star outline set this pot apart from others (809).

We have seen only one cricklight, a later adaptation by Samuel Clarke of his patented fairy night light. He registered the trademark in 1889. They decorated dining room tables when used as a candelabrum (810).

Heavy cutting did characterize many of these pieces. This hanging flower vase, complete with chain, combined hobstars with bands of cane (811). A light fixture bowl came with the necessary chains for hanging (812).

No one needs to make you a list of rare pieces. You will soon learn to recognize them when you look for the unique in cut glass.

808. A coffeepot with a flat base and detailed cutting.

809. A coffeepot in a star outline with a shaped base, decorated spout, and notched miter lid.

810. A cricklight by Samuel Clarke, used on tables as a candelabrum.

811. A hanging vase complete with chains.

812. A light fixture bowl with band and hanging chains.

EXCEPTIONAL PIECES

When you look at these pieces, you most likely will say, "Wow! Would I like to own one of them!" The three-part epergne in Russian leaves no question as to its inclusion in this classification (813).

Large trays offered the designer opportunity to express his artistry. In this round tray the star outline blended perfectly with the shooting stars (814). Decorative bars framed flashed stars with hobstars in the points (815). This oval tray combined flashed pointed loops of Russian with hobstars (816).

Large orange bowls seemed to challenge the pattern maker's creative ability. To find two large shapes in the same ornate pattern proved exceptional. This orange bowl has the same pattern as the oval tray (817). The size, the crimp rim, and heavy cutting created a super piece in another orange bowl (818). Russian between the points of the star outline and the cane and notched miter bars made a third orange bowl a marvel of design (819).

These treasures have no identification except beauty, possibly the best reason for existing. Never give up hope that some day we may find the pattern name. Even if you never identify an exceptional piece of cut glass with characteristics similar to these, you will still experience the pleasure of owning or seeing a true treasure.

813. A three-part epergne in Russian and a pair of candlesticks in a notched prism pattern.

814. A 16-inch tray in a star outline.

815. A 14-inch tray in a bar outline and unique stars.

816. An 18-inch ice cream tray in a very rare pattern.

817. An 11½-inch orange bowl in the same pattern as the ice cream tray shown in 816.

818. A 14-inch orange bowl in Gothic arches and hobstars.

819. A 14-inch orange bowl in a combination pattern of star and Gothic arches.

8

Reflections on Glass

WHENEVER collectors and dealers gather informally and discuss certain subjects about cut glass, disagreements develop. We have researched original and secondary sources on a number of these subjects. Perhaps these reflections based on our research will help you in buying or selling cut glass.

POLISHING

In the early years of the Brilliant Period, craftsmen polished by hand the whitish cast caused by cutting the glass. Hand polishing consisted first of using a wooden (willow) wheel with pumice or other abrasives on the major miters or large cuts. Several types of brushes containing an abrasive restored brilliance to the smaller cuts. This worked very well with simple patterns, such as this comport (820).

At the height of the Brilliant Period when patterns became more ornate as in this ice tub (821), brushes could not remove all the white from the minute

820. A comport that needs only hand polishing.

821. An ice tub that would require acid and hand polishing.

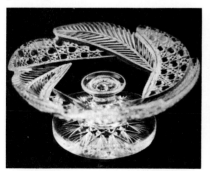

cuts. The companies discovered that dipping the piece into an acid bath removed the whitish cast on parts difficult to reach with a fine brush. This process also saved time and money. The length of time the piece stayed in the acid bath proved crucial.

If the piece stayed too long in the bath, the acid left a watered look on the miters and clear parts. You can easily detect a poor acid polish by closely examining a piece. Egginton did his own acid polishing. Miss Egginton has said that when he dipped the pieces in the acid, he recited a nursery rhyme as a timing device. Unfortunately, no one asked which verse he recited. His glass showed a very fine acid polish, but he probably finished the job with some hand polishing.

Most major companies followed the acid bath with hand polishing on the clear parts and large cuts to remove any watery appearance. More and more authorities agree that the finest and sharpest pieces resulted from a combination of acid and hand polishing. Any number of ornate patterns needed this procedure.

REPAIRS

Sooner or later someone will bring up the subject of repairs. Some purists say, "No, never!" Dealers will frankly state, "Try to sell a damaged piece." A person who does repairs suggested, "Why let your fingers get cut when you can remove chips and flakes?"

Each individual must make the decision in regard to repairs, but consider these facts. We inherited a vase in a star outline and hobstar motif with a missing foot. Later we found a matching foot in the flea market of Mexico City, offered for sale as a paperweight. Donald Parsche converted the broken vase and odd foot to a very lovely lamp we use and enjoy (822).

An enterprising dealer, for example, took a broken plate in Panel by Hawkes and converted it to a fan which he used as an eye-catcher in his booth at antiques shows. We never recommend that you convert a lovely vase or pitcher to a lamp or make any other similar changes. But if we can restore a damaged piece to usefulness or remove sharp chips and ugly flakes, we do it.

This does not mean go to the extreme in repairs and create a new shape. We have a friend who has collected some obviously repaired pieces, such as a single-handled sugar. Other conversions include changing a broken carafe into an odd rose globe, a base of a tubular vase into a "wine coaster," and removal of a handle on a punch cup to make a handleless one. If you know the basic shapes of cut glass, you can easily recognize such adapted pieces.

Above all, watch out for those very rare items that repairs change into rarities. A rare footed bowl resulted from a reshaped fern (823). A fan-shaped vase emerged from a basket with a broken handle (824). Obviously, the repairman could not bring himself to remove the handle on this decanter, so he created a "hanging rose globe" (825).

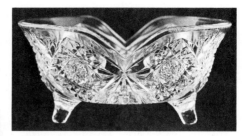

823. A repaired fern.

824. A fan-shaped vase made from a flower basket.

822. A broken vase converted to a lamp.

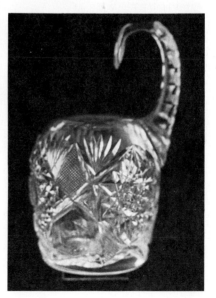

825. A "hanging rose globe" created from a decanter.

MATCHED AND MARRIED PIECES

"Marriages" occurred easily with American cut glass because the companies cut pieces in standard sizes. Stoppers have a high casualty rate so replacements occur frequently. Most stoppers contained a number that matched the same one on the neck. Any time a stopper rocks in the neck or goes in too deeply or too shallowly, beware of a replacement. Mismatched numbers will prove this.

Some replacements fit perfectly because of standard sizing, so you must rely on other tests, such as shape. A Worcestershire bottle required a stopper with a flat cap. The stopper in this bottle belongs to an oil (826). The whiskey jug came with a cylinder stopper (827). Oils came with a long neck stopper and colognes with a short neck one. If the piece has a decorated stopper, make sure that it matches the body. The stopper on this coffeepot does not match and goes too deeply into the neck (828).

A second type of mismatching consists of the marriage of the same shape but different patterns. Always check two-piece items for matches: plates under butter or cheese covers, butter or ice tubs, mayonnaise or salad bowls. We have heard people insist that two part punch bowls in different patterns came from the factory that way.

One woman wrote us that she owned a lovely lamp with three signatures: a Libbey on the dome, Fry on the foot, and Dorflinger on the silver. Someone did a tremendous assembly job and created a many-company splendor. Lamps and punch bowls get married more often than other pieces. The foot and the first globe match on this lamp, but the second globe has a different pattern (829).

826. A Worcestershire bottle with a stopper for an oil.

827. The whiskey decanter used a cylinder stopper.

828. The stopper on this coffeepot does not fit nor does the pattern match.

829. The parts to this lamp do not match.

MINIATURES AND SALESMAN'S SAMPLES

A collector of miniatures will frequently bring along the so-called physical evidence that a company produced salesman's samples. Miniatures and salesman's samples seem to refer to any small object that duplicated the shape of a large piece of cut glass. We questioned cutters and members of families associated with the production of glass, and none had ever heard of salesman's samples.

As soon as you mention them, people visualize a person carrying around a case of small objects from which buyers placed orders. To the contrary, the catalogs served this function. Donald Parsche has stated, "Some companies gave away small pieces as gifts when receiving a large order. I know Libbey did it." He went on to explain, "My father gave a paperweight as a bonus with a large order for bar bottles and decanters." Paperweights also come under the whimsey classification (830).

When workers made whimseys, they could have created pieces similar to this whisk broom in Strawberry-Diamond and a very different fan (831). Other small pieces companies gave away or sold at national or international fairs. Some of these, most likely, contained the signature of the company.

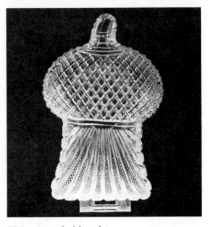

830. A typical paperweight.

831. A probable whimsey.

Companies did produce doll dishes in cut glass, as was done in old pattern glass. These included a teapot, sugar and cream, covered butter, plates, and cups and saucers. We have seen one such set in cut glass complete with the original velvet-lined case. In addition Dorflinger cut children's bread and milk sets that came in special boxes. While the size seems a little large, some may designate them and odd creams to sugar and cream sets as miniatures. The butter plate and cover came in a set of children's dishes (832).

Wrong identification has kept the theory of salesman's samples alive. Two fancy individual salts, one with applied and the other with built-in handles, have been identified as miniature nappy and ice tub. Another collector showed us a miniature in the shape of a leaf but listed as an individual nut dish in a Hawkes catalog. As previously mentioned, some call violet vases miniature flower centers and an individual olive dish a miniature celery.

Tourists bring back some of these cut glass miniatures from Europe. The poor cutting gets excused because of the small size. Any time that you purchase a miniature or salesman's sample, know what you buy.

832. A butter cover and plate from children's set of dishes.

LARGE OR SMALL PIECES

Many collectors will tell you, "I buy only the large pieces." Another will say, "I buy small pieces because I don't have too much space to display glass." By all means buy what you like or have space to display. If you ignore some interesting small pieces, you will miss some good buys.

Reprints of old catalogs illustrate many of these small items. By studying a catalog, we recognized a bargain in a flat toothpick holder in cane (833). Another collector found this toothbrush bottle in panels of single stars and crosshatched diamonds (834) and the soap dish or pin tray in hobstars and notched miters (835). Various collectors have found some interesting small items, such as a Strawberry-Diamond matchholder and ash receiver (836) and a cigarette lighter in notched miters (837). We envied the person who found this all-glass syrup in hobstars and fans (838).

Even with limited space, you can find room for at least one large item. Choose an outstanding piece: a punch bowl (839) or a large tray (840).

833. A flat toothpick holder.

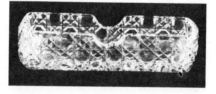

834. A toothbrush bottle.

835. A soap dish or pin tray.

836. Match holder and ash receiver.

837. A cigarette lighter.

838. An all-glass syrup.

839. A footed punch bowl.

840. A large ice cream tray.

841. Flared ale or iced tea tumbler.

Do remember that companies added new shapes with changes in social customs. Several added new shapes to tableware. The catalogs listed cocktail and champagne tumblers—not juice glasses. Several companies cut tall flared tumblers for iced tea or ale (841). Handled lemonade glasses became most popular after 1900. Teddy Roosevelt ordered highball glasses for the White House. Libbey introduced creme de menthe and hors d'oeuvre sets. Companies cut grapefruit glasses with liners. When you know about these la' additions, you can often find a sleeper.

Do think in terms of sets, such as matching saucers to the berry bo tumblers to a carafe or jug. A cocktail set contained a quart and pint dec mixing tumbler, cherry jar, bitters bottle, and tumblers. Collecting piece by piece, offers quite a challenge and satisfaction when you hav pleted it.

A plateau, a rounded mirror with silver trim, went with various s plateau may lie flat or have feet. The silver trim varied from plain t For the most decorative plateaus, the craftsman also cut a borde mirror. Many of these plateaus done with silver plate will need rest this costs only a nominal fee. Nothing so compliments a bowl, con or punch bowl as a silver plateau.

RECORD KEEPING

Even though you have only a few pieces, you need to keep them. We use a 4-by-6-inch file card:

```
SHAPE:                                              No.

IDENTIFICATION (by signature, pattern, or description):




CONDITION AND REPAIRS:


SOURCE AND COST OF ITEM:


CURRENT VALUE BY DATE
```

Under identification list the name of the company that signed the piece, the pattern if known, possibly the location in a published book, and a description. In writing a description note the function and size; then describe the pattern and any extra features in this manner:

> An oval relish dish in Creswick signed by Egginton, 8½ inches long, has a scalloped sawtooth edge and step cutting on the extended handles at either end. Hobstars fill the spaces between the crosshatched points and the center of the star outline (842).

When you describe the condition, mention chips, flakes, poor color, or any other defects. If you have the piece repaired, tell where and at what cost. Then evaluate the repair job.

You may want to clip the sales slip to the card and also a photograph. Do give the date purchased, where, and at what cost. Make sure that you add the cost of any repairs.

Every two years redate the card and give a new value to the piece. You can use the back of the card to adjust the value. This file card can simplify an appraiser's job when you insure a collection.

238

842. A relish dish in Creswick and signed Egginton, catalog identification.

INSURANCE

For a nominal fee, most insurance companies can attach a fine arts endorsement to your household goods policy. Contact your insurance agent for the exact amount.

You will need to supply the agent with a list of the pieces, their condition and current replacement value, and a description or book reference. An appraiser or dealer of cut glass can verify the values of pieces in your collection. Annually or semiannually, you should update the list, adding new pieces or withdrawing those you have sold, traded, or given as gifts. When giving a gift, add a photograph and a description for the new owner.

Insurance covers any damage to your glass. A piece may crack in a cabinet or disappear. You or another person may break something. This insurance coverage refers only to glass in a private collection and not that for sale in a shop. Such insurance costs much more.

CLUB OR ORGANIZATION

"I'm not a joiner," you say. Maybe not, but you can learn much from others who collect cut glass. Most clubs or organizations print a monthly newsletter with researched information, meet monthly, or hold national conventions. Inquire about a club or organization in your local area at the public library or the chamber of commerce. The American Cut Glass Association, an international organization, was organized in 1978. It holds an annual convention in different areas of the United States and publishes a monthly newsletter. By becoming a member you will gain more than you give in knowledge and friendships.

SELLING A COLLECTION

A person may decide to sell a collection for various reasons: death of the collector, a move to a smaller house or apartment, or the need for money. You may sell a collection in a number of ways.

Advertise in a newspaper or antiques magazines. This may work perfectly or could set you up for a robbery. If you advertise, give only your telephone number, and try to screen the prospective buyers.

Professional sellers will take over a collection for a fee or a percentage of the sale. They work by appointment only and show the collection to interested persons they know. You may locate such professionals through a club or the American Cut Glass Association. Or write to a columnist on glass and antiques. This way you need check the reputation of only one person.

Sometimes you can sell your cut glass through a club or organization. You price the items at market value. A collector will usually pay 75 percent, while a dealer will offer approximately 50 percent of the market value, depending on the quality of the glass. Dealers must pay shop upkeep while they wait to find a buyer. If you want a quick sale, you may contact a dealer of cut glass and sell the entire collection for a lump sum.

Finally, you can sell at public auction. The auction house takes a percentage of the selling price. Some houses let you set a reserve price, meaning that the item cannot sell for less than a certain amount. Do know exactly the terms of the sales agreement.

You can choose one of these methods or use all of them. Your choice depends on the number of items for sale and the amount of time you can afford to spend. Do investigate all means of selling before you make a decision.

The research on cut glass never ends. With museums, glass club members, and those of the American Cut Glass Association searching for old catalogs and any old records on the American Brilliant Period of cut glass, new information appears frequently. Meanwhile share your cut glass by displaying it attractively or using it for special family occasions as your parents and grandparents did. Yes, even trade some for more wanted pieces. Above all else, treasure your American cut glass; you own the finest in the world (843).

843. Lamp in Russian.

Appendix A. Signatures

SIGNATURES ON AMERICAN RICH CUT GLASS

C. G. ALFORD & COMPANY
New York, New York

J. D. BERGEN COMPANY
Meriden, Connecticut

ALMY & THOMAS
Corning, New York

T. B. CLARK & COMPANY
Honesdale, Pennsylvania

M. J. AVERBECK MANUFACTURER
New York, New York

C. DORFLINGER & SONS
White Mills, Pennsylvania

O. F. EGGINTON COMPANY
Corning, New York

HUNT GLASS COMPANY
Corning, New York

H. C. FRY GLASS COMPANY
Rochester, Pennsylvania

IORIO GLASS SHOP
Flemington, New Jersey

T. G. HAWKES & COMPANY
Corning, New York

IRVING CUT GLASS COMPANY
Honesdale, Pennsylvania

J. HOARE & COMPANY
Corning, New York

LACKAWANNA CUT GLASS COMPANY
Scranton, Pennsylvania

HOBBS GLASS COMPANY
Wheeling, West Virginia

LAUREL CUT GLASS COMPANY
Jermyn, Pennsylvania

HOPE GLASS WORKS
Providence, Rhode Island

LIBBEY GLASS COMPANY
Toledo, Ohio

LYONS CUT GLASS COMPANY
Lyons, New York

PITKIN & BROOKS
Chicago, Illinois

MAJESTIC CUT GLASS COMPANY
Elmira, New York

SIGNET GLASS COMPANY
Address unknown

MAPLE CITY GLASS COMPANY
Hawley, Pennsylvania

H. P. SINCLAIRE & COMPANY
Corning, New York

NEWARK CUT GLASS COMPANY
Newark, New Jersey

STERLING GLASS COMPANY
Cincinnati, Ohio

PAIRPOINT CORPORATION
New Bedford, Massachusetts

L. STRAUS & SONS
New York, New York

P. X. PARSCHE & SON COMPANY
Chicago, Illinois

TAYLOR BROTHERS
Philadelphia, Pennsylvania

TUTHILL CUT GLASS COMPANY
Middletown, New York

THE VAN HEUSEN CHARLES COMPANY
Albany, New York

UNGER BROTHERS
Newark, New Jersey

WRIGHT RICH CUT GLASS COMPANY
Anderson, Indiana

**NATIONAL ASSOCIATION
OF CUT GLASS MANUFACTURERS**

UNIDENTIFIED SIGNATURES

Hoehke   *Mitchell*   J.W.H.

     Mc D BROS

     ASH BROS.   OM^EG^A

    M(A   *ELLIS*

CANADIAN CUT GLASS SIGNATURES

HOUSE OF BIRKS
Montreal, Canada

GOWANS, KENT & COMPANY LIMITED
Toronto, Canada

GUNDY, CLAPPERTON COMPANY
Toronto, Canada

PORTE & MARKLE

RODEN BROTHERS

PATTERN NAME	COMPANY	ILLUS. NUMBER
Baker's Gothic	Clark	224
Baltic	Bergen	535
Basket	Hoare, Libbey, Hawkes, Pairpoint	558
Bellevue	Taylor	485
Bengal	Sinclaire	407
Bengal & Engraving	Sinclaire	408
Berkshire	Empire	258
Berlyn	Quaker City	75
Bermuda	Bergen	214
Berwick	Pairpoint	380
Blackberry	Tuthill	553
Block Diamond	Pairpoint	384
Boston	Pairpoint	733
Brilliante	Dorflinger	234
Bristol	Sinclaire	403
Brunswick	Alford	458
Brunswick	Hawkes	511
Burgundy	Alford	457
Butterfly	Niland	714
Butterfly & Daisy	Pairpoint	756
Butterfly and Flower	Tuthill	763
Cambria	Egginton	119
Cambridge	Hawkes	284
Camelia	Clark	229
Cane		112, 182
Canton	Hawkes	285
Cape Town	Averbeck	460
Carolyn	Hoare	319
Carolyn	Pitkin & Brooks	387
Castilian	Egginton	245
Cecil	Hawkes	283
Cherry	Libbey	751
Cherry Blossom	Libbey	750
Chicago	Fry	264
Chrysanthemum	Hawkes	494, 495
Chrysanthemum (Gravic)	Hawkes	740
Clarendon	Clark	218

PATTERN NAME	COMPANY	ILLUS. NUMBER
Clarion	Clark	522
Classic	Gundy-Clapperton	490
Clifton	Pairpoint	378
Cluster	Egginton	550
Cluster	Tuthill	425
Cobweb	Hawkes	544
Colonna	Libbey	343
Columbia	Blackmer	73
Columbia	Libbey	359
Combination Rose	Irving	469
Comet	Hoare	324
Comet	Libbey	147
Concord	Blackmer	462
Constance	Hawkes	280
Constellation	Hawkes	711
Corinthian	Hoare	506
Corinthian	Libbey	505
Cornell	Pairpoint	377
Covina	Dorflinger	235
Creswick	Egginton	496, 842
Criterion	Alford	456
Croesus	Hoare	323
Crystal City	Hoare	326
Cut & Engraving No. 1	Sinclaire	413
Cut Rose	Tuthill	742
Cyprus	Hawkes	292
Dahlia	Tuthill	427
Daisy	Mt. Washington	738
Daisy	Pairpoint	757
Daisy	Tuthill	768
Deer	Hawkes	309
Delaware	Hawkes	84
Denver	Sinclaire	409
Derby	Pitkin & Brooks	390
Devonshire	Hawkes	515
Diamond Point	Tuthill	439
Diamonds & Silver Threads	Sinclaire	415, 416

PATTERN NAME	COMPANY	ILLUS. NUMBER
Gladys	Hawkes	521
Glenwood	Bergen	212
Gloria	Maple City	477
Goldenrod	Bergen	210
Gotham	Hoare	312
Grapes, Cherries, and Pears	Tuthill	774
Grecian	Hawkes	123
Greek Key	Libbey	202
Harvard	Clark	222
Harvard	Hawkes	291
Harvard	Libbey	518
Heart	Pitkin & Brooks	545
Hiawatha	Sinclaire	401
Hobart	Unger	454
Hob and Lace	Dorflinger	232
Hob Diamond	Dorflinger	231
Holland	Hawkes	295
Homer	Clark	228
Hudson	Hawkes	548
Hunter	G. W. Huntley	571
Huyler	Clark	516
Imperial	Hawkes	513
Imperial	Hawkes	514
Imperial	Libbey	78, 356
Imperial	Straus	422
Intaglio Grape	Tuthill	434
Iorio Special	Empire	259
Isabella	Empire	252
Isabella	Libbey	339
Iris (Gravic)	Hawkes	743
Japan	Empire	542
Japany	Hoare	542
Jersey	Clark	225
Kaiser	Hawkes	288
Kenmore	Libbey	358
Kensington	Libbey	361
Keuka	Hawkes	297
Kimberly	Libbey	507
Kings	Hawkes	510
King George	Fry	263

PATTERN NAME	COMPANY	ILLUS. NUMBER
Kohinoor	Hoare	525, 526
Korea	Pairpoint	535
Kremlin	Empire	351
Lake Lamoka	Hawkes	310
La Rabida	Straus	423
Laurel Wreath	Parsche	480
La Voy	Unger	451
Leaf	Hawkes	281
Leota	Libbey	341
Lilliaceae	Tuthill	435, 676
London	Averbeck	461
Lorraine	Hawkes	304
Lotus	Egginton	551
Magnolia	Mt. Washington	369
Manhattan	Empire	255
Marcella	Libbey	360
Marlboro	Dorflinger	66, 67, 68, 106
Marlborough	Quaker City	395
Marie	Bergen	207
Marquis	Hawkes	512
Marquise	Egginton	242
Marquise	Hoare	316
Mars	Hawkes	282
Mars	Pitkin & Brooks	385
Mayflower	Clark	221
Melrose	Libbey	365
Mercedes	Clark	227
Mercedes	Wright	713
Meteor	Hoare	317
Milano	Pairpoint	371
Minton	Hawkes	296
Monarch	Hoare	547
Mont Clare	Clark	217
Morning Glory	Tuthill	764
Murillo	Pairpoint	755
Myron	Luzerne	476
Myrtle	Pairpoint	379
Mystic	Quaker City	397
Napoleon	Hawkes	302
Nasturtium	Tuthill	771
Nautilus	Hawkes	523

PATTERN NAME	COMPANY	ILLUS. NUMBER
Plaza	Pitkin & Brooks	121, 540
Plum	Tuthill	450
Plymouth	Empire	541
Poppy (Gravic)	Hawkes	742
Poppy	Libbey	746
Poppy	Pitkin & Brooks	101
Poppy	Tuthill	436
Potomska	Pairpoint	381
Premier	Bergen	206
Primrose	Quaker City	391
Primrose	Tuthill	440, 442, 443
Primrose and Bar	Tuthill	441
Primrose and Swirl	Tuthill	444, 445
Prince	Empire	537
Princeton	Liberty	474
Prism	Egginton	248
Prism	Libbey	334
Prism	Pitkin & Brooks	389
Prisms	Sinclaire	398
Progress	Bergen	215
Queens	Hawkes	509
Queenston	Roden	492
Quilted-Diamond and Star	Tuthill	424
R. C. Arctotis	Sinclaire	758
Raised Diamond	Pairpoint	383
Ramona	Pairpoint	376
Redmond	Blackmer	463
Regal	Blackmer	538
Regal	Sterling	484
Regina	Hawkes	272
Regis	Libbey	337
Renaissance	Clark	531
Renaissance	Dorflinger	531
Renaissance	Pitkin & Brooks	513
Rex	Tuthill	503
Riverton	Quaker City	549
Rockmere	Monroe	540
Roland	Pitkin & Brooks	541

PATTERN NAME	COMPANY	ILLUS. NUMBER
Roosevelt	Quaker City	396
Rosaceae and Flowering Raspberry	Tuthill	433
Rose	Clark	516
Rose	Libbey	745
Rosemere	Tuthill	769
Rosette	Tuthill	426
Royal	Dorflinger	237
Royal	Empire	554
Royal	Libbey	331
Ruby	Blackmer	464
Russian	Dorflinger	233
Russian	Hawkes	18
Russian	Mt. Washington	267
Russian	Unger	113
Russian	Unknown	16, 719, 843
Russian and Border	Sinclaire	412
Russian and Pillars	Hawkes	275
Salem	Pairpoint	373
San Gabriel	Clark	543
Saratoga	Pairpoint	372
Saturn	Sinclaire	399
Saxonia	Empire	552
Sciota	Fry	266
Senora	Libbey	345
Seymour	Bergen	50
Shell	Tuthill	428, 429, 430
Sherwood	Egginton	246
Signora	Hoare	314
Silver Leaf	Pairpoint	374
Silver Rose	Tuthill	760
Snowball	Clark	709
Snow Flakes and Holly	Sinclaire	410
Split and Hollow	Bergen	533
Star	Pitkin & Brooks	539
Star and Hobnail	Phoenix	482

PATTERN NAME	COMPANY	ILLUS. NUMBER
Starling	Blackmer	44
Stars, Pillars and Engraving	Sinclaire	405
Steuben	Hoare	318
Stratford	Libbey	338
Strawberry (Gravic)	Hawkes	744
Strawberry Blossom	Tuthill	772
Strawberry-Diamond	Pairpoint	382
Strawberry-Diamond	Unknown	177
Strawberry-Diamond and Fan	Hawkes	124, 270
Strawberry-Diamond and Fan	Unknown	102, 109
Success	Empire	716
Suffolk	Hawkes	721
Sultana	Dorflinger	240
Sultana	Libbey	347
Sunburst	Pitkin & Brooks	388
Tasso	Bergen	209
Temple	Buffalo	554
Thistle	Hawkes	741
Thistle	Hawkes	277
Thistle (Gravic)	Hawkes	741
Three Cut Octagon	Pairpoint	528
Tokio	Egginton	247
Touchstone	Gundy-Clapperton	488
Trellis	Egginton	529
Trellis	Hoare	529
Trieste	Alford	538
Troy	Blackmer	537
Teutonic	Hawkes	307
Two Cut Octagon	Pairpoint	554
Typhoon	Empire	253
Ucatena	Pairpoint	370
Undine	Unger	453

PATTERN NAME	COMPANY	ILLUS. NUMBER
#98	Sinclaire	404
#100	Libbey	346
#100	Sinclaire	419
#104	Fry	265
#114	Fry	711
#125	Libbey	362
#11-136	Empire	257
#142	Fry	311
#175	Fry	545
#205	Libbey	340
#207	Libbey	363
#221	Libbey	342
#233½	Fry	260, 261
#251	Roden	491
#300	Libbey	352
#307-9	Roden	365
#411	Libbey	366
#643	Dorflinger	544
#1021	Sinclaire	418
#1189	Hawkes	300
#1284	Hawkes	306
#1286	Hawkes	303
#1903	Libbey	355
#3708	Hawkes	528
#5336	Hoare	211
#9921	Hoare	543
#10711	Marshall Field	569
#76045	Marshall Field	570

PATENT RECORDS

31781	Gibbs, Kelley & Co.	702
32150	Clark	701
32210	Meriden	703
32211	Meriden	704
35323	Straus	705
36739	American	699
36865	American	700
81788	Straus	706

Bibliography

Avila, George C. *The Pairpoint Glass Story*. New Bedord, Mass.: Reynolds DeWalt Printing, Inc., 1968.

Boggess, Bill and Louise. *American Brilliant Cut Glass*. New York: Crown Publishers, Inc., 1977.

Daniel, Dorothy. *Cut and Engraved Glass 1771–1905*. New York: M. Barrows and Company, Inc., 1950.

————. *Price Guide to American Cut Glass*. New York: William Morrow & Co., Inc., 1967.

DiBartolomeo, Robert E. *American Glass*. Princeton, N.J.: Pyne Press, 1974.

Ehrhardt, Alpha. *Cut Glass Price Guide*. Kansas City: Heart of America Press, 1973 (contains 8 catalogs).

Evers, Jo. *The Standard Cut Glass Value Guide*. Paducah, Ky.: Collectors Books, 1975 (contains 5 catalogs).

Farrar, Estelle Sinclaire. *H. P. Sinclaire, Jr. Glass Maker* v. 1. Garden City, N.Y.: Farrar Books, 1974 (contains inventory photographs).

———— and Jane Spillman. *The Complete Cut and Engraved Glass of Corning*. New York: Crown Publishers, Inc., 1979 (contains inventory pictures of Sinclaire glass).

Fauster, Carl U. *Libbey Glass*. Toledo, Ohio: Len Beach Press, 1979.

Hotchkiss, John F. *Cut Glass Handbook and Price Guide*. Des Moines, Iowa: Wallace-Homestead Book Co., 1970.

Kovel, Ralph M. and Terry H. *A Directory of American Silver, Pewter, and Silver Plate*. New York: Crown Publishers, Inc., 1961.

McKearin, Helen and George S. *American Glass*. New York: Crown Publishers, Inc., 1946.

Mebane, John. *Collecting Bride Baskets*. Des Moines, Iowa: Wallace-Homestead Book Co., 1976.

Newman, Harold. *An Illustrated Dictionary of Glass*. London: Thames Publishing Company, 1977.

Oliver, Elizabeth. *American Antique Glass*. New York: Golden Press, 1977.

Padgett, Leonard. *Pairpoint Glass*. Des Moines, Iowa: Wallace-Homestead Book Co., 1979.

Pearson, J. Michael. *Encyclopedia of American Cut and Engraved Glass*, 3 volumes, Miami Beach, Fla., 1975–1977.

_____ and Dorothy T. *American Cut Glass For Discriminating Collector*. New York, 1965.

_____ and Dorothy T. *American Cut Glass Collections*. Miami Beach, Fla., 1969.

Rainwater, Dorothy T. *Encyclopedia of American Silver Manufacturers*. New York: Crown Publishers, Inc., 1975.

Revi, Albert Christian. *American Cut and Engraved Glass*. New York: Thomas Nelson & Sons, 1965.

_____. *The Spinning Wheel's Complete Book of Antiques*. New York: Grosset & Dunlap, 1972.

Schroeder, Bill. *Cut Glass*. Paducah, Ky.: Collectors Books, 1977.

Stevens, George. *Canadian Glass, 1825–1925*. Toronto: Ryerson Press, 1967.

Warman, Edwin G. *American Cut Glass*. Uniontown, Pa.: E. G. Warman Publishing, Inc., 1954.

Weiner, Herbert, and Freda Lipkowitz. *Rarities in American Cut Glass*. Houston: Collectors House of Books Publishing Co., 1975.

CATALOGS

Alford Cut Glass, 1904.

Averbeck Rich Cut Glass: catalog #104.

Bergen Cut Glass Company: 1904–1905, 1907–1908.

Blackmer Cut Glass: 1904, 1906–1907.

Buffalo Cut Glass Company catalog.

T. B. Clark & Company: 1896, 1901, undated, 1905, 1908.

C. Dorflinger & Sons: catalog #51, 1881–1921.

O. F. Egginton Company catalog.

Elmira Cut Glass Company catalog.

Empire Cut Glass Company: 1906, 1910, 1912.

H. C. Fry Glass Company catalog.

Gundy-Clapperton Company: 1909, 1915.

T. G. Hawkes & Company: 14 catalogs of Brilliant Period, two late catalogs, and advertising booklet.

Higgins & Seiter: 1893, 1899.

J. Hoare & Company: three catalogs with no dates, 1911 catalog, and undated scrapbook.

G. W. Huntley, 1913.

Irving Cut Glass Company, Inc., catalog.

Keystone Cut Glass Company catalog.

Kranz & Smith Company catalog.

Lackawanna Cut Glass Company: two catalogs.

Laurel Cut Glass Company: two catalogs: one 1907, other undated.
Libbey Glass Company: 1893, 1896, 1898, 1904, 1905, 1908, 1909, 1900–
    1910, c. 1920.
Liberty Cut Glass Works catalog.
Linford Cut Glass Company catalog.
Lotus Cut Glass Company: No. 49, No. 50.
Luzerne Cut Glass Company: two catalogs with no dates.
Maple City Glass Company: 1904 #3, 1906 #5, 1911 #10.
Meriden Cut Glass Company catalog.
C. F. Monroe Company: #6, other undated.
Mt. Washington Glass Works: 5 catalogs of Brilliant Period.
Niagara Cut Glass Company: two catalogs.
Ottawa Cut Glass Company, 1913.
Pairpoint Corporation: possibly five catalogs.
Parcel Post Cut Glass Company catalog.
F. X. Parsche & Sons Company catalog.
Phillips Cut Glass Company catalog.
Phoenix Glass Company: 1893 and undated one.
Pitkin & Brooks: 1907 and undated one.
Powelton Cut Glass Company catalog.
Quaker City Cut Glass Company: two catalogs undated.
Rochester Cut Glass Company catalog.
Roden Brothers, 1917.
Sterling Cut Glass Company: two catalogs.
Steuben Glass Works catalog.
L. Straus & Sons, 1893.
Taylor Brothers: two catalogs.
Tuthill Cut Glass Company, The Connoisseur.
Unger Brothers: two catalogs: 1906 and undated one.
Unidentified Salesman's Catalogue, 1890–1905.
Unidentified catalog, possibly Hoare.
Wallenstein Mayer Company, 1913.

Index

Page numbers in *italics* refer to illustrations.
Page numbers in **boldface** refer to main references to makers.